MW01107998

Robyn Watson

LIGHTCROW

MESSAGES

with

Antoine

Robyn Watson

LIGHTCROW MESSAGES with Antoine

Copyright © 2011 Robyn Watson

ISBN-10: 1499386168

ISBN-13: 978-1499386165

DEDICATION

I would like to dedicate this book to *Arkala...She Wolf*...my Animal Spirit Guide and protector, who has watched over me constantly...throughout this lifetime, and throughout all others.

I honor you my dearest friend, and I thank you for agreeing to be my travel companion once again.

I would also like to thank my beautiful and loving family for their continued support and encouragement. It would not have been possible for me to have undertaken this journey without it.

To my Husband: *You are my rock, and I continue to Love you in both worlds.*

To my two Daughters...my closest friends: *Helping to bring two such incredibly gifted and beautiful Souls into this world is a privilege and an honor. I Love you both more than you could ever imagine.*

To my two beautiful Granddaughters: *You are so courageous for simply being here, and you are both so incredibly special. I Love you beyond belief.*

To my future Grandchildren: *I know that I have met you on the other side of the veil, and I look forward with great anticipation to the day when I can greet you on this side, and welcome you into this world. I Love you already.*

I am indeed blessed!

CONTENTS

PART ONE

PART TWO

ACKNOWLEDGEMENTS

My gratitude and Love goes to Richard Dana...not just for his editorial skills with this work, or his profound creative skills manifested within the creation of this book cover, but for all that he is, and for all that he has brought to my life.

My eternal gratitude and Love also to Antoine and Lightcrow...without their Love and encouragement, this book would simply not have been written.

INTRODUCTION

Through the process of finding my own Truth, I have recently come to the understanding that my Soul purpose for this lifetime is one of Support for Humanity, as a Teacher and Lightworker... someone who creates a space to allow the Light of Love and Truth to filter through, and to spread to others who might seek it. Through this process, I have discovered my own gift of channeling. As the physical author of this work, this has allowed the wisdom contained within these pages to be passed on to you...a much wider audience; however, the true authors of this work are *Antoine* and *Lightcrow*.

My own life has been transformed in unforeseen and miraculous ways since I have been working with them on this level, and I will always be grateful. We all have this gift; we all possess the innate ability to channel. We simply have to open our minds and our hearts to connect to it, and then leave the window wide open!

The Gifts from *Antoine* were initially given to me as guidance to help me personally; he is one of my Spirit Guides.

Lightcrow is a Master Teaching Guide; he has come through in this way to spread his message on a much wider scale.

I am indeed honored.

Our beloved planet is taking an evolutionary leap, and we as the Human species are undergoing a huge shift of consciousness at this time. As the Earth ascends into Her new position of alignment within the higher dimensions, which is necessary for Her own evolvement, Her vibrational frequency, or energy is rising, and because we have chosen to remain within Her vibration, so too must ours. Our energy is beginning to vibrate at a much higher frequency than ever before, and our physical body is changing, in order to accommodate more of our Light Body. Because of that, we are more able to access and carry the new, lighter energies that are now available to us from the universe, and what has been previously hidden from us, or what we chose to forget when we incarnated on this beautiful and unique planet is now being revealed to us, on a conscious level. This means that we are beginning to see, hear and feel things from the higher dimensions that only a few of us have been able to access in the past. Because of this, our whole way of thinking and of interacting with Mother Earth and each other is changing. This must be allowed to take place; otherwise, She will not continue to support us; She will simply evolve without us!

I must point out that within my level of understanding, the dimensions are not places. They are in fact, different levels of vibrational energy, or consciousness. I believe that we are moving away from the third, which is individual consciousness, passing through the fourth, which is a stepping stone or a bridge, and moving on into the fifth, which is unity consciousness. We, along with everything else that exists in the universe are comprised of energy, and that energy can never be destroyed. Our energy is no different to electrical energy, which requires a circuit to be returned to the source...the power grid. Our physical body is that circuit, and this is what happens to our energy when our physical body can no longer sustain us. Our consciousness returns to the power grid...The Source...The One Consciousness. We never really die; we always have existed, and we always will exist.

This is simply the way it is.

There are many others like me, who have agreed to be here at this time as Teachers and Healers, and as Support Crew to help people understand these concepts, and to help them remember who they truly are.

Some of my own journey has been woven throughout the beauty and Love within these pages. My hope is that by sharing it with you, I might help others, who are having similar experiences, but do not understand what is happening to them. It is often hard to talk about with other people, especially in certain sectors of our society where such experiences are still ridiculed by many people. These people have not yet opened their minds and their heart centers wide enough to understand, and they simply know no differently. If something in these words brings some degree of understanding and encouragement to someone on their own spiritual journey, and in so doing helps them to reveal the hidden treasure of their own Truth...then I shall feel blessed indeed.

I wish you well on your own journey.

I wish you Love.

PROLOGUE

Born a child of the early fifties, I was blessed with fairly strict, but loving parents. Hardly the type of parents who understood the spiritual aspects of life though, and this caused conflict between us during my growing years. They did not understand me at all! I was aware from a very young age that there was much more to this world than one could actually see, but I did not understand it. I understood even less why people behaved towards each other in the way that they did.

Drifting off to sleep at night, I could often feel a distinct presence. Sometimes an unseen hand would hold mine, and quite frankly, I was terrified! I was afraid to go to sleep because I was convinced that there was a physical presence in the room with me, and for some reason, I was simply unable to see it. Consequently, I would seek solace, but would invariably be told that it was all in my imagination and to just go to sleep, so that everyone else could get some sleep as well! I shared a bedroom with my older sister, and my younger brother was in an adjacent room, so their sleep was also disturbed. I just could not understand why any other family member didn't realize that there was somebody else in the house with us!

Why was it just me?

My parents sought medical help for my sleeping problem, and I was eventually prescribed a vile tasting medicine, which was to be taken at bedtime. It was supposed to make me sleep, but in fact had little effect. I would remain in a waking state for most of the night, crying and upset until one parent would eventually take pity on me and move into my bed while I slept with the other one in theirs. Some nights this was the only way any of us got some sleep, and it must have been extremely upsetting and frustrating for my family, to say the least.

I could not explain to anyone what my problem was because I did not really understand it myself, and I was too afraid to talk about it; however, I did begin to understand that I had an incredibly strong mind. I could even override a sedative if I wanted to...that much was obvious! I was also aware that I had the ability to "see" things before they actually happened. This was quite scary for me, and I would become anxious wondering when certain events I already knew about would eventuate. I learned very quickly to keep all these things to myself because to share would have invited ridicule. I already had a sense of low self-esteem because I knew that I was different to the other people around me.

This situation plagued me for most of my growing years until finally, as a teenager, life took over, and I began to block those aspects of my reality out. I settled into some sort of normality as I then saw it, but even then I felt as though I did not fit in anywhere. In fact, I always felt quite alone because I also found it difficult to make and maintain friendships.

I was born in the small, Northern New South Wales town of Bangalow, as my Father had been before me. My family was actually living in Byron Bay at the time of my birth, but the hospital there had not yet opened. I lived an idyllic life by any child's standards, enjoying the surf and the magical beaches almost daily until the age of six when my Father took a transfer with Australia Post, as it is now known, to Townsville in North Queensland. This decision was made partly for our education needs because we would have had to travel quite a distance when we reached high school level. It was also made for my Mother's benefit because her family was in Charters Towers, and my Grandmother was not well. This is when I first remember experiencing my sleeping problems.

To add to my anxiety, we were often the target of a prowler, or more correctly, a peeping tom. There were in fact, two of them...one younger and one older. Each of them would come on to our property at different times at night, and attempt to open up our wooden louvers at the back of the house, or peer through any open windows at my sister and me. Even in the extreme heat, we felt that we could not safely leave our casement windows open at night, and because our house was lowset, we were an easy target for them. Understandably, as a young girl, I was extremely frightened about this, and I would become anxious towards nightfall.

Eventually, the Police had patrol cars checking our house at regular intervals throughout the night, but the offenders obviously lived very close by. They seemed to know when the cars had been around because the problem continued, and they were never caught in the act. My Father almost caught one of them one night, but he was much younger and bigger than Dad, and he pushed him to the ground while making his escape. Although it was too dark to be sure, Dad had his suspicions, so he confronted one of our back neighbors, but of course the accusation was denied. Soon after this though, the incidents ceased, but it all contributed to my fear, and I was quite literally afraid of everything…seen and unseen!

I have always instinctively known that I was following a certain path, even though I had no idea what that path was, or where it was leading me. I have made decisions throughout my life that even I didn't understand, so how could my family and those around me possibly understand. Even though I was reasonably smart at school and could have easily furthered my education, I had absolutely no inclination to follow a career path. I left school at sixteen and worked in the credit office at Woolworths before finding employment as a receptionist-nurse at a suburban Doctor's surgery. I was comfortable with the work, but one of the Doctors intruded on this enjoyment. It is enough to say that he delighted in making my life a misery with his disrespect and control tactics. I have chosen not to re-visit this particular experience because it was so difficult.

I eventually felt that I had no other option than to leave, so I returned to my previous employment. Soon after though, I changed direction on my path and relocated to Brisbane. I kept working in similar positions until my first Daughter was born, and then I became a full-time Mum. My second Daughter was born almost three years later. When she started school, I more or less fell into the position of Diversional Therapist in a residential aged care facility. I worked mainly with the residents experiencing Dementia and Alzheimer's disease, and I loved it! I had finally found my niche, and I continued working in this role for many years.

When I was twenty years old, I ended a long term relationship with my boyfriend, whom I adored. He was my best friend, but after he had betrayed my trust, I felt devastated, and I was simply unable to work things out with him. I do regret the way things were left between us and today I would perhaps handle the situation a bit differently. He will always hold a very special place within my heart.

I felt an attraction for someone at my place of work, and I finally said "Yes" when he asked me to marry him. He was European, and I had convinced myself that I was "In Love" with him. I think perhaps that I may have actually been "In Love" with the romance of a wedding more than anything! By the time the wedding was due to take place, I knew that I was not "In Love" with him, but for some inexplicable reason, I just knew that I had to go ahead with the marriage. Much to my parents' understandable upset and disapproval, I left him after just three weeks! Just as surely as I knew that I had to marry this man, I also knew that I must get as far away from him as possible. I sensed in him a danger for me that I could not define, and my instinct was right. Without going into detail, I will simply state that I was entirely right to follow my intuition. I have a strong suspicion that he may have already been married in his own country anyway, and I doubt very much that his marriage to me was even legal.

I had to pay for a divorce anyway!

When our car broke down while travelling to our new home in western Queensland, a Good Samaritan stopped to help us, and he actually took us the rest of the way in his car. He was also the one who helped me escape from my new husband, and at some point along the way, we fell into a comfortable relationship. We eventually married, and he is the Father of my two beautiful Daughters. I will always Love him, and to this day we remain good friends. We were happy for eighteen wonderful years, but I always felt a sense of something missing from my life. We would probably still be together if fate had not stepped in and played her hand.

I now understand that what I perceived as fate at that particular time was actually a part of my Life Blueprint being played out, and in fact, everything that has happened in my life has been a part of what I planned before I chose to incarnate on this beautiful planet. Everything that has happened was designed to happen, so that I could be led to this exact point, at this exact moment in time.

At the age of thirty-eight, my life was thrown into complete chaos when my present husband entered my life. Literally in a heartbeat, the sense of something missing dissolved, and my life was changed completely. I can honestly vouch for the fact that Love at first sight is entirely possible, but this was much more than that. The only way I can try to describe what I experienced is to equate it to riding on a speeding roller coaster...one that it is impossible to exit. I had the sense of being pushed forward at an alarming rate, and I was simply not in control of the situation! Not only was my life thrown into chaos, but also the lives of the ones I loved the most. I knew that I was responsible for their pain, but there was simply no way that I could not be with this man. Believe me, I tried to walk away and so did he, but our Souls had recognized each other the instant we met, and from that moment on, our fate was sealed. We knew each other in a way that neither one of us could articulate. At that moment, my spiritual awakening began, and he became my mentor. For the first time in this lifetime, I knew what being "In Love" felt like, and I could not let it go. I had to follow my heart...my Truth!

That was almost twenty-one years ago. In some ways it seems like yesterday, but during that time there has been much emotional pain and sadness, as well as much healing taking place, and I would like to think that everyone involved has reached a place of understanding and forgiveness. During this time, I received a lot of condemnation and judgment from a number of people, who somehow believed that it was their right to do that, and in fact, some of them made every attempt to make my life a living hell. Of course they never had the right to make that judgment because they were not walking in my shoes...they were not me!

It was simply not their experience...it was mine.

In retrospect, I simply handled the whole situation in the best way possible with a sense of Love and respect for everyone involved. Believe me, it would have been much easier for me if I had not done that! The best possible outcome was always my intention.

My life since then has not been an easy one. I have faced many different challenges throughout the years, and I continue to do so, but I do not regret my actions, or the decisions I made for an instant, because that was the beginning of my spiritual awakening, and within that awakening, I discovered my own Truth.

I discovered who I truly am.

I discovered why I am here.

PART ONE

CHAPTER ONE

Introducing Antoine

first became consciously aware of Antoine`s presence in late march of 2010...a few weeks before my 58th birthday. I now understand that he has always been with me, supporting and guiding me since birth. I now realize that it has been his vibrant, masculine voice that I have heard physically on occasion over the years, offering words of wisdom to me at times when I have needed it most. His has also been one of the voices I have heard while I have been experiencing an altered state of consciousness. At these times, he has been discussing the state of the world as it is today, and what Humanity needs to do about it.

I have always silently talked my problems through to myself, and I believe guidance has come to me in this way on many occasions. I have often felt the soft, gentle presence of someone with me at these times, but afterwards I would question it. I wondered whether it had simply been my imagination, and I was merely talking to and answering myself.

I have done this my entire life.

This time it was different.

I was not quite awake one morning, and I was pondering a particular problem I was experiencing on a personal level when a voice began interacting with mine. It was not a physical voice like I have heard on occasion. It is very hard to describe adequately, but this was an audible thought process in my mind, which held a distinctly male energy, and it appeared to be emanating from my right ear area. The closest way I can describe it so that it can be understood is by imagining in your mind a favorite song that is being sung by the original artist. You don't physically hear it like you would if you had the radio turned on listening to it, but you are hearing that person singing it in your mind...through your thought process. I asked him if I wasn't imagining this could he please tell me who I was speaking with. I was immediately told: *Antoine.* I wasn't sure if I had heard the name correctly, so I asked him to spell it for me. He actually showed me the written name in my mind. There was no questioning it!

During this first interaction, he spoke with me on a personal level. He told me that he was one of my personal Spirit Guides and he has always been with me. He said it was time to help prepare me for the work I had agreed to do with them…my writing. I have known for a long time that one day I would write. I have four journals spanning fifteen years, which are filled with documentation of my dreams and visions, and also my encounters with different spirit entities during my out of body experiences. I have also been visited in visions by other spirit people, telling me and showing me that I will write books someday. At times I have become impatient, and I have asked when this would take place. The answer that I always believed I heard through my thought process has always been the same: *Patience Child!*

Although I have always loved reading and writing, and I felt that I had a reasonable command of English, I had never attempted to write a book, and I knew absolutely nothing about the publishing process. Apparently, this is what Antoine was going to assist me with, but first he wanted to work with me on some personal issues so that I could be totally focused on the important work ahead.

Our second session later that same day was a surprise to me to say the least, although in retrospect, it shouldn't have been. It was the same male energy and the same voice, but this time there was a distinctly French accent attached. After all, wasn't his name a French one? I asked him why he was now speaking to me with a French accent. He told me that he wanted to "jog" my past life memories. This, I totally understood! I have had memories and dreams of a life lived in France before and during the Second World War. These memories also involve my present day husband. I have always felt very connected to everything French, and I was even given a French name by one of my Spirit Guides for my first Granddaughter, which she now bears. My eldest Daughter also has a French Spirit Guide. I asked him a few questions about himself, but he said that he didn't want me to focus too much on him; however, he did want me to know that there was a strong past life connection between us, and I would soon understand more about that. In this session, he spoke to me about many personal issues, and his words have brought some clarity and understanding to my present situation.

The next time we communicated, his French accent was absent. I asked him why this was because I had rather enjoyed listening to it! He told me that the purpose had been served, and there was now no need to use it. Since then, we speak constantly. Our exchanges have become quite rapid, and he seems to be answering my questions before I have even finished asking them. It is now almost like thought transfer taking place between us. I only have to say his name, or ask if he is there, and he immediately answers: *Yes Child.* I asked him if he is always with me, and he answered: *Always Child.* He always refers to me as: *Child.*

Antoine has brought me many beautiful teachings concerning specific Human emotions; these include the aspects of: Love, Happiness, Hope, Fear, and Trust. He has also brought through his beautiful thoughts on Helping and Making a Difference. This has been especially helpful to me because it is something that I have been struggling with recently.

When I expressed my surprise and wonder at the fact that we could communicate so readily. He said: *Why are you surprised Child?* And I quote: *"Heaven and Earth are as one. There are no barriers... only increasing Light!"*

I was intrigued with the fact that he and I had shared a recent past life connection, and as I was thinking about this one evening while working on my computer, I suddenly felt compelled to run a search on his name. I just as quickly thought how ridiculous that idea was because I assumed that *Antoine* was a fairly common French Christian name, and a search would probably

achieve nothing; however, Antoine had other ideas. I
heard his words coaxing me: *Just do it Child! It can't
hurt can it?* I typed in his name, and then clicked on
search. I was surprised to find so many different names
listed there, but one of them virtually jumped from the
page at me, and my heart raced. I decided to look at all
the others first, and leave that particular name until last.
Most of the names were obviously French, but there were
no bells ringing for me with any of them. Finally, I clicked
on the name I had deliberately left until last, which was
also very obviously French, and I felt goose bumps all
over! Rarely have I experienced such exhilaration; it was
total, instant recognition!

What were the odds that this incredibly gifted and
celebrated man, who was also regarded as a Hero, and
called this Earth his home for the first half of the
twentieth century was indeed my Antoine? I had never
even heard of him! I asked him if he could please verify
the fact that this was indeed him. I received a somewhat
vague answer stating that for the moment, he didn't want
me to focus too much on him or his last lifetime. The
important thing was that I understood our connection,
and the work we would be doing together. I should make
up my own mind about it…end of conversation; however,

I could sense him smiling!

As I read the many websites dedicated to this French Hero, I realized that I was crying, and there was no doubt in my mind that somehow I had shared a part of that life with him. There were too many similarities between his life and my past life memories, and there was also the fact that he had been a writer. Can I prove this? Of course not, but in my heart, and in my Soul, I know it to be my Truth, and as Antoine told me a long time ago, on one of those occasions when I heard a physical voice, which I now know to be his:

The Truth is all there is!

As I write these words, my mind drifts back to another time when I heard this same physical voice. It was the first time I ever heard it; it was a time more than twenty years ago when my life was in chaos. I was wondering out loud whether Spirit Guides really did exist, and who mine might be because I certainly needed one! The answer came quickly and loudly, and I jumped in fright. Just two words in a loud, masculine voice: *A Hero!* At the time, I didn't understand. I ask him now why he has left it so long to identify himself properly to me. His answer: *You simply weren't ready Child!* Straight and to the point!

Antoine, if I may borrow one of your phrases: *I am indeed happy and humbled to be working with you at last.*

Note: At this particular time, for the purpose of this writing, I have not properly identified Antoine by stating concisely who I believe he was during his last incarnation on Earth. This is his wish, which I have honored. We understand the relationship between the two of us...past and present, and that is all that is necessary. His belief is that for this work, it is the messages he brings through that are of the most importance, and not who the messenger might once have been while in physical form.

He emphatically states that he has already experienced his time of notoriety on this planet!

CHAPTER TWO

Introducing Didi

A few weeks following Antoine's initial contact, I was speaking with him when I became aware of a second presence interacting with me. This presence was distinctly female, and Antoine was obviously aware of it also. He seemed quite happy for her to communicate with me while he was present; in fact, they appeared to be together. She introduced herself to me as Didi, and she told me that she was also with me on a personal level. She said that she was helping me with all aspects of the feminine...me, my Daughters, and my Granddaughters because there was so much feminine energy around me. My family is very distinctly female! She said that she was bringing help, understanding and healing to these relationships, and she was also bringing in the female energy to balance my relationship with Antoine. She told me that I have seen and spoken with her on other occasions during my visions and out of body experiences. At these times she has brought me guidance; apparently, she is the one I documented in my journal a long time ago. I wrote her name as Dodi at that time, but she reminded me that at the time I wasn't sure if I had heard her name correctly. I remember that I did think it was Didi, but couldn't remember exactly, as often happens when I return from an altered state of consciousness. I remember writing Dodi because I was familiar with that name, and I had never heard the name Didi before.

She said that she had been a member of Antoine's family during their last incarnation together; she was still his family in spirit, and so was I. She said that they were a part of my Father's spiritual family, and they were very happy to be communicating with me like this at last. She also told me that although I perceived them as separate entities, they were in fact, all a part of the One. Didi comes through to me with the energy of an older woman, and she calls me...*Dear.*

Journal: February 1st 2000

Towards morning, I drifted into an altered state of consciousness, and I found myself being shown an array of books in what appeared to be some sort of catalogue. I was being shown three, beautifully bound, gold colored books when I realized that someone was with me. I looked to the right of me and saw a middle aged woman with short, dark, wavy hair; she was wearing a short sleeved, blue and white frock. She smiled at me, and I asked her who she was because she seemed vaguely familiar to me. I thought that she said her name was Dodi, but I questioned it because I wasn't sure if I had heard it properly; it sounded like a strange name for a woman! She said it again, and then she told me that it was important that I remember it. I asked her how long she had known me. She smiled and said: All my life; even when I was a young boy! She disappeared, and in my half asleep state, I kept saying the name over and over in my mind so I wouldn't forget it. I even materialized a pen and paper and tried to write it down, but every time I tried, the letters came out differently. Finally, I brought myself back to my waking state, and then I actually got up and wrote it on a piece of paper.

Note: In retrospect, it is now obvious to me that the reason the name kept manifesting differently when I was writing it down was because she was trying to tell me that I had gotten one of the vowels wrong, and her name was in fact, Didi. Earlier in November of 1999 during an altered state of consciousness, I was shown a set of small format books. They had beautiful drawings on the covers, and each one was titled: *Zen* with a subtitle underneath. Each of them was about an aspect of Human life, such as: Birth; Death; Passion; etc. I never understood what that meant until Antoine started bringing similar teachings through to me.

Journal: October 4ᵗʰ 1998

Lucid dream last night: I was in an old house with another young woman, and we both saw the heavy cream curtains at the bedroom window move. It was a bay window I think, and I have had bay windows in my bedrooms before. I moved to close the window, but then I realized that the window was already shut. As we both watched, a fine mist began forming from the center of the curtains. The other girl looked horrified! I told her not to be afraid because it was just something manifesting, and then a tall, silver spirit entity, which was almost translucent appeared. It moved across to me, and then it handed me a sheath of papers with something folded in the middle of them; I think they were photos and paper clippings. The entity told me that it was most important that I publish them. Just before it disappeared, I asked it what they were and why it was important, but it didn't answer me. It just repeated very emphatically that I must publish it, and it was of the utmost importance. I remember looking at the papers, and I saw that there was writing on them, but I don't remember what the writing was about.

Journal: March 21st 2000

I felt myself entering an altered state of consciousness and started to pull back a little, but then I felt a tremendous pull to keep going. After a moment, I felt the presence of someone there with me, and I realized that I was with a very attractive looking male spirit entity. He had smooth olive skin with black wavy hair and the deepest blue eyes. He held me close to him, and I could feel immense Love and comfort radiating from him. I asked him who he was, but he didn't answer me; he just smiled instead. All of a sudden he was gone, and I was transported to a different place. I found myself with someone else, but I think that he must have taken me there.

I was with a young woman with short, wispy, pale ginger colored hair and a sprinkling of freckles. I felt that

I knew her, so I asked her who she was. She told me that I would find her name in the Bible. I asked her if her name was Rebekah because I saw that name flash into my mind; she just smiled at me. Suddenly, she materialized my "Teddy Bear Box" where I keep all of my journals and writing. She started going through my books with me and pointed to one particular extract I had written. She told me that I thought I had written it, but in fact, it had come from them. Apparently, a lot of what I write does come from them, and now I must learn to become more consciously aware of the fact that they are guiding my writing.

As I told my husband about the visitation, I wondered how on earth I was going to find her name in the Bible because I knew that it was full of female names. I wasn't even sure if I had heard her name correctly. He reminded me that I had a very old, family Bible in my cupboard that had belonged to my Great Grandfather; it had been given to him by my Great Grandmother. He suggested that I take a look at it because there were also inscriptions with family names inside it, including dates of births and deaths. When I opened it, I saw my Grandmother's name there, along with the names of other female family members, but somehow I didn't feel that it was any of them. There has always been a little crochet bookmark in the shape of a cross between some pages inside the Bible, and I have no memory of ever moving it for as long as it has been in my possession. I opened it where the bookmark lay and it read: *GENESIS 24 25.* There on the left hand page at the top was written: *ISAAC MEETETH REBEKAH.* I just couldn't believe it! The spelling was even the same as I had seen it in my mind.

Journal: December 20th 2008

Lucid dream early this morning: I was at some sort of marketplace and my husband was with me. We must have been on holiday or something because he told me that I should buy just one small thing to remind me of it. I told him that there was really not much there that interested me, but just at that moment I happened to look over and saw a glass cabinet full of exquisite little ceramic figurines. I was drawn to a beautiful figurine depicting a crab. It was in muted colors of purple, pink and green and had small pearls for its eyes. I went up close to the cabinet, but all of a sudden the glass disappeared, and so did all the other figurines in the cabinet. I reached out and picked up the crab. As I handled it, I realized that its claws were segmented and they moved; it was just like a real crab. My husband told me to take it into the shop nearby to pay for it because there didn't seem to be anywhere around the cabinet to pay. We assumed that the cabinet must have belonged to the adjacent shop.

I went in and a dark haired woman approached me straight away. She was middle aged, and I think she wore glasses; she also seemed vaguely familiar to me. She told me that the crab looked lovely on me. As I looked down, I realized that it had transformed and was now draped across my chest like a top to wear with a skirt or pants. She said that she had lots of beautiful clothes to show me, and then she proceeded to bring out different items of clothing. I told her that I wasn't interested in clothing…I just wanted to buy the crab. She virtually ignored me, but then she asked me to please follow her and she would show me something that would really suit me. As we passed a wide doorway leading into the back of the shop, I stopped to look in and saw a large room filled with lots of wooden bins. Each bin contained different types of writing materials, but some of them also contained stacks of blank books. The woman turned towards me and asked me how long I had been living where I was, and what I had been doing with myself. I told her that it had been almost three years and I was really doing nothing in particular, but I was ready to start doing something now.

She just looked at the books, and then she turned and smiled at me.

Note: Not long after this dream, I realized that the woman in it had actually reminded me of my Mother, who had worked for most of her working life in a women's fashion retail store. My Mother's birthday was July 8th and in Astrology terms this equates to Cancer... the crab!

Maybe this was my darling Mother, appearing to me as some other aspect of her Soul, and she was giving me a gentle reminder. Perhaps I was being told that it was time for me to start preparing for my writing!

CHAPTER THREE

Gifts From Antoine

Antoine first brought through his beautiful teachings to help me...to bring me guidance and comfort on a personal level. For that, I will always be grateful; however, I am becoming increasingly aware that his words might also bring that same measure of comfort to others, especially in these very troubled times in which we have chosen to live. Along with his blessing, many of his gifts to me are now being passed on to you. I am selfishly keeping the deeply personal ones locked away in my heart, for they were for me alone. Our hope is that something in these words may speak to you personally, and perhaps bring you comfort in some way.

That is our wish.

Helping and Making a Difference

There are many of you helping and making a difference at this time, but there are also many of you who are not. Helping connects you to each other and to your planet. Your Loved One understands this and so do you, so why do you hesitate? We know that great Love abounds within you, but you must open up your heart to allow it to do its work. You have so much to give...so much my Child! You must believe in yourself as we do; we come to help you with this. You must unlock the gate of fear and embrace the beauty beyond. Only you can do this, but we can help by guiding you. Open your heart to us and allow us to do our work...then step fearlessly through the gate. You will never have regret, and you will find great reward; we will never leave your side. We are so happy to have your ear at last, for now we can begin our work together. Trust Child! Many need your help also. Tread carefully in Love and you shall not be shunned...only good comes.

Me: I hesitate because I am afraid of things happening to myself, or the ones I love.

Antoine: That is not your path. That is the path of others who have chosen it. You are simply there to help and support them.

Forever the skeptic, I asked Antoine for some kind of physical confirmation that this was indeed coming from him, and I wasn't just making it all up! It was a Sunday, and I was just about to get to the Sunday paper. I made myself a cup of tea and read the main part of the paper, and then I opened up the Sunday Magazine. There inside on the second page was an article titled: *Making a Difference.*

Point taken!

I posed a question to Antoine about my indecision to stay where I was, or to move on.

Fear and Trust

If you are afraid, you cannot trust. Trust that we are here at all times, protecting and helping you. You have asked for and manifested your home and environment. You know this Child. Now it is up to you to use it the best way you can. If it is not working for you and you are not happy…then make yourself happy! Simply try something different and move on! Your work can be done anywhere, and your Loved One's work is needed everywhere, but remember also that you are needed where you are. *Trust minus Fear equals Faith.*

You must understand this Child.

Hope

Hope is necessary for human survival; *Hope plus Faith equals survival.* Without hope, the Human spirit may have a tendency to give in…to fold, so to speak. Even in the darkest hours, if there is even just a tiny spark of hope, survival is possible. Without this spark, the Light of Faith cannot take hold and burn brightly, lighting the way through the darkest tunnel. All Human pathways encompass these dark tunnels, but the Light is always there, waiting to embrace you at the other end; it has never really been extinguished. Never give up hope Child! We are always with you, guiding and holding that Light with you. It has always been this way.

You are never alone. You know this Child.

Self-doubt

Self-doubt is your greatest obstacle. You know this Child. When self-doubt creeps in, you are in danger of being overwhelmed by all manner of negative emotions. Isn't this so? This happens when you don't trust yourself…when you don't have enough faith in yourself. Know that you are capable of anything and of everything.

You only have to believe it and it is already done. Believe in yourself Child. You must believe, for it is only with this belief that great things are achieved...your potential reached, so to speak.

Past Lives

Think of this life as you would a series running on your television screen. Each week there is an episode of the same program. Each is separate, but also a part of the whole...a continuation, so to speak. Each lifetime is like one of those episodes; each is separate, but a continuation of the one story...your story, and that story never ends. You have always been, and you will always be. This is simply the way it is.

You know this Child.

Happiness

Just as you say beauty is in the eye of the beholder, so too happiness is in the heart of the beholder. What encompasses happiness is unique for each Soul. When the life led is in communion with the Soul purpose...then happiness follows. Every Soul has a reason for being in physical form...something they are working on...a project if you like. The reasons for this are always to do with Soul growth. Whatever you choose to do in your life; whether you are a parent, or a great teacher, or a healer; if it is aligned with your Soul growth, it will bring happiness. No purpose means any less than another. When you are within this alignment, your life will flow freely and easily, and when you are not, you will experience unhappiness and discontent. This will soon overflow into all areas of your life. When this happens, you will know that it is time to make different choices. We are happy to give guidance throughout this process, but you must take the action needed. Often, this requires a great deal of courage on your part, but know that this is the path you chose while planning this lifetime. You are only following the path of your Truth. Step up and step forward in Faith, for it is already written...already done.

You know this Child.

Anger

Anger is a most negative Human emotion. It wastes energy, causing destruction on many levels of the Human spirit; it serves no useful purpose. Anger is not in alignment with any Soul purpose, which is always growth. To learn to Love; this is the real purpose...the ultimate purpose of Soul growth. Anger and Love cannot. co-exist; to truly Love is to forgo anger and forgive instead. When anger is replaced with forgiveness and understanding, only Love can exist; forgiveness is the ultimate act of Love.

You know this Child.

Realization

Realization is simply the physical manifestation of thought. First there comes the thought, and then the intention. The action that follows allows the realization, or physical manifestation to take place. This is true for everyone in your world because you exist in a world of matter...of lower vibration. In our world, only the energy of thought is necessary. You are manifesting everything in your life continually...every second of every day. If you are not happy with certain aspects of your life, this can be altered...simply think different thoughts. Change your way of thinking, and put new thoughts into process. This is not always easy for you, but it is the only way. If you think only positive thoughts and truly let go of the negative, only transformation can take place, and only the actions of Love can follow. This will truly bring happiness. This is simply the way it is.

You know this Child.

Truth

The Truth is all there is. The Truth is all that matters because it is all that is real in your physical world. Everything else is only there to help lead you to the Truth. They are only the tools, which you have manifested, in order to help you experience the world of matter in which you have chosen to live. The ultimate Truth is that only Love matters; the ultimate truth is Love. Each one of you will eventually learn this. Whether it is during this lifetime or another, you will all learn this, and it will be the ultimate knowing and recognition of the Truth. When you experience only Love, you will understand; you will have understood the ultimate lesson, and you will have no reason to return.

You know this Child.

Guidance

You all have guidance originating from these planes of existence to help you along your chosen path. Many of us are making contact with you at this time. This becomes easier for us as your vibration rises to become more in tune with ours. The veil between our worlds of existence grows thinner. The Light grows brighter for many of you because you and your natural world are evolving rapidly towards that Light. We have an agreement between us before you enter into physical form...a pact, so to speak; you also have free will. Sometimes the two are at odds with each other. Often the ego, or personality part of you, or Human part if you like will try to override this guidance. You may take a few, or many detours before you eventually return to the main path, but you will... never doubt that. We go to great lengths to ensure this. You will follow your chosen path. It is already written; it is already done. When you have taken the last step, your mission will be completed, and you will happily return Home to us once again. We are here to help you; you only have to be still, and to be aware and listen.

You know this Child.

Hate

Hate is like anger. It is the darkness that is the opposite of Love, and it is a most negative Human emotion. It serves no purpose except to destroy, but if this is on your path, you must learn this lesson. Hate not only affects the Soul the vibration is projected towards, but it also affects your own Soul because the two are connected. Make no mistake about this! All matter is comprised of the same essence...the same energy, and this includes you! If you hurt anything or anyone...emotionally or physically, you are ultimately hurting yourself. You will also have to pay the price. All thought, word and deed attracts Karma. What you would judge as good or bad Karma is entirely up to you. Judgment is purely a Human condition. For us everything is simply experience, but the effects cannot be bypassed by any one of you because it is the natural way of things...the natural law. This is simply the way it is.

We know you have learned this Child.

Angels

We are indeed happy and humbled to speak with you about this most magnificent of beings. Angels are indeed everywhere, and they are happy to be called upon by you at any time. They exist within the highest levels of consciousness, or vibration, and have never incarnated in Human form. They are neither feminine, nor masculine as you understand gender, but may appear to you as either. They can manifest in Human form, or any other form they choose. To some, they may appear as magnificent winged creatures, and to others differently, but they have never been born into a Human body as you have done. We know that you have experienced them and resonated with them in your own deeply personal way Child. Angels do indeed walk amongst you! They come in times of need when called upon, but will also draw near to help when a life is in danger, and it is not yet time for that Soul to return home. You may also call on Angels on behalf of another. They love to listen to your prayers, but a formal prayer ritual is not necessary to invoke their help. You only have to form the thought and they are with you instantly. Each of you has an Angel companion with you throughout your earthly lifetime; these you refer to as Guardian Angels. They never leave your side, and they assist you with every aspect of your life. They love nothing more than to be acknowledged by you. Speak with your Angels and include them in your consciousness. Miracles can and do happen!

You know this Child.

Journal: August 5th 1996

Last night I found myself in the company of two entities, which I perceived as Angels. They were beings of Light, and they were emanating pure Love. They were vibrating at a very high frequency, and emitting what I can only describe as angelic music. It was like nothing I have experienced before. It was emanating from their whole being, and it is impossible to describe adequately. I suddenly realized that the same music was emanating from me, and as I looked down at myself, I realized that I looked just like them…I was all Light, and I was vibrating with them in time with the music. I have never before experienced such Love. I remember seeing what I can only describe as gossamer like filaments of colored Light around their perimeter, which one could certainly perceive as wings.

I have also met my Guardian Angel, who introduced himself to me as Darius. I have communicated with him on a number of occasions now, but the first time was an experience I will never forget.

Journal: March 27th 2005

I went to bed last night feeling upset because I was not able to spend my elder Granddaughter's birthday with her today; they are now living too far away from us. Early this morning, I had an encounter with a beautiful, male spirit entity, who introduced himself to me as Darius. He appeared to be rather feminine looking with blond curls, intense blue eyes and very clear skin, and he radiated intense Love and trust; it was an incredible experience. He took me out of body to see my Granddaughter, who was also out of body. I remember hugging and kissing her, and wishing her a Happy Birthday; she was laughing, and I was so happy.

I came back crying!

I believe Darius to be my Guardian Angel.

Passion

Just as food is fuel for the body, so too is passion fuel for the Soul; passion adds Love to the equation! Without this Love, aspects of your life might become mundane and meaningless. Each Soul feels the need to be passionate about something in their physical life. Whether it is a Loved One, an activity, or some great cause, it is always to do with Soul growth. None is of lesser value than another. What are more important are the process, the emotion, and the experience. Do not confuse passion with obsession...the two are very different. Obsession can be destructive to the Soul. Passion motivates the Soul, and it is an accelerator for Soul growth. Be aware that there can sometimes be a fine line between the two.

You know this Child.

Awakening

Many of you are waking up at this time; you are one of these Child! You are moving into a new higher level of consciousness, and this can be very unpleasant for you because it requires you to have a new way of thinking and of being. Many of the old aspects of yourself are being shed, just as a butterfly sheds its cocoon when it has been transformed into the magnificent creature that it always was. These old ways will not serve you as well in the New World that is now emerging. You are rising in consciousness along with Mother Earth Herself in a magnificent display of color and enhanced vibration, which we are witnessing from our vantage point! Your very purpose for this incarnation is at hand! You and many others have agreed to help turn the tide on your planet from one of greed and self-service to one of Unconditional Love, and peace and abundance for all of Humanity. So it shall be; it is time! We know you experience physical symptoms that can be disturbing for you at times, but these will pass as your physical body comes into alignment with your new, higher vibration. The new way of being will be incredibly exciting for ones such as you, but others will find it extremely frightening because they will find it impossible to let go of their emotional and physical attachments. These will need your help during this shift in Human consciousness. We are here to help you, and we know that you are up to the task, for it is already done!

Depression and Self-harm

Depression is, simply put, a disconnection from the Divine. For whatever reason, the Soul partly disconnects from the Source, and it does not feel the full connection and support of the universal Light and Love. With some, this condition may be mild and temporary, and with others, it may be more severe and ongoing, but it is always a condition of the Soul. When the Soul is able to reach out, we are many who are able to work to help alleviate the distress, but the main work is done by the Soul itself because it is often this condition that is the trigger for the Awakening. This is Soul work! Depression as you call it is not necessarily a negative condition and something to be avoided at all costs; it is often Soul growth at its best!

Medications prescribed by your physicians may only slow down, or prevent this important work from occurring, and they may also hinder our supporting role. The Soul will in most cases find the way back again on its own, and become one with the Source once again, stronger and ready to advance further.

This process has been spoken of by your scholars as "The Darkness of the Soul" and "The Night of the Soul," and that is exactly what it is. It is a disconnection from the Light...from The Divine!

Sadly, in some cases this feeling of disconnection becomes so complete that the Soul feels that it has only one option, and that is to return to the Source...to the Light and Love once again to be healed. It may feel helpless and abandoned and doesn't understand that it may only choose to return again to complete the process. It may also need much help and Love and healing on this side of the veil to adjust, but whatever the reason may be for self-harm, help will always be offered and given if accepted, (free will always prevails) to bring it safely back into the Light; to connect once again with the Divine!

Love

Once true Love flourishes between Souls, it can never be lost, for it is absorbed into the deep consciousness of the Soul and remains there for eternity. You speak of many forms of Love, romantic included, and indeed, the personality of the physical being thinks that it experiences these, but all Love is of the one strand...Love is Love. It all emanates from the One Divine Source. Think of it as like a brilliant, beautiful diamond cut into many facets. Each facet has its own unique brilliance, but there is really only one diamond. Love is the whole; it is really all there is. Love is all that matters, and only Love is real in your world of illusion. The vibration of Love is the Essence; Love is the Light; Love is the opposite of Fear and the darkness.

You know this child.

Re-membering

Just as you chose to wear the veil of forgetfulness when you incarnated on your planet of free choice, you can also choose to lift it and remember who you truly are. Many of you are choosing to do this at this important time. Many of you have chosen to remember that you are in fact, spiritual beings of Light...of pure energy, and you have come to Planet Earth to help raise the Planet and all that exists with Her into a new dimension...a higher dimension with a higher vibration and frequency. This is the most important of work!

We from these dimensions honor your work, and we watch with great anticipation! Your physical bodies are being changed, or "re-wired" to accommodate more of your divine Energy...your Essence; only a small part has been accommodated within your physical body in the past. This is allowing you to vibrate at a frequency much more in tune with your Higher Self and All That Is. You are lifting your veils, and you are allowing yourselves to *consciously* communicate with all beings in the universe, including your Higher Self, which is that vast part of you still existing outside your physical body.

You are truly incredible Creators, and we are honored to be a part of your creation.

Reality

Each Soul creates and projects an extremely intricate holographic reality. This is what makes each of you different and unique in the world of matter. You have created everything about you...your entire universe. Because of that, you each view everything differently... from a different perspective. As you lift the veil of forgetfulness, you are beginning to understand the world of illusion you have created, and you are beginning to see who you truly are. As you begin to understand that everything and everyone is actually connected, the illusion of being separate will fall away. You will realize that you are not different...you are not separate. You will realize that each of you has created everything from the one essence, and this is the essence of All That Is. You are all no different to the natural world around you. Even those things you perceive as solid and inanimate with no life-force are composed of this same energy.

You know this Child.

Harmony

Your Soul is consciously seeking out those images and sounds that resonate with the same vibration as your own. This is called Harmonic Resonance. When you find and feel these vibrations around you; you are instantly attracted to and in tune with that harmonic, and you resonate with it; you interact in accord with each other. Nothing is more natural, or more beautiful than this attraction. This does not just apply to people. It is the way of everything around you, including your surroundings and your animal companions...everything! To live this way is to live in balance and in harmony. It is magical!

You know this Child.

Re-connection

Souls who have made contracts on this side of the veil will sometimes meet and connect early in their incarnations. Most of you are only aware of this on a subconscious level because you have chosen to wear the veil of forgetfulness. Although there may be no physical contact for a long time (within your understanding of time) while each of you completes other work you have chosen to do, contact continues between you on a super-conscious level...that vast part of you that is not encompassed within your physical being, but remains connected to you, as well as to the hum of the universe... the All That Is. Reconnection takes place at critical times when that contact is needed to honor the contract. Sometimes this will be fleeting, and sometimes it will be ongoing, but it is always valuable and necessary for the evolvement of the Soul.

We reach out to you from this side of the veil to help facilitate this process, and to help you to remember.

We know that you feel our Love and encouragement Child.

We honor you and the work you do with us.

CHAPTER FOUR

My Recent Soul Re-connection

Not long before Antoine brought me his insight on reconnection, I felt compelled to search out old school friends on a well-known social site. I don't know why because from a young age, I have instinctively known that I had a different path to tread. I always felt different, as though I didn't fit in anywhere... not even within my family.

I have always believed in leaving the past behind because the past is the past, and it is finished, or so I thought! I was about to learn something entirely different. Since communicating with Antoine in this way, I have begun to release much of my old way of thinking, and I have recently felt an unusually strong need to reconnect in some way with my past. There were only a few people I recognized from my leaving year listed on the social site, but one of them stood out from the rest for me because I had known him best.

After procrastinating for a few days, I decided to bite the bullet and make contact. I expected that he might not even remember me because it was so long ago, and if he did, I would at the most become just a face on his friends list. I could not have been more wrong, and I will never regret the decision I made that day. I will always be grateful for the guidance that led me back to a very special connection...a special friend, and I thank him for his trust and acceptance of me back into his life so readily. I also thank his beautiful family for allowing me to be a part of their lives as well.

I have been amazed by this incredible turn of events, and as we catch up on each other's lives, we are both struck by the parallel course our paths have taken over the years. We were incredibly close to meeting again on more than one occasion, and the amount of so called coincidence in our lives is striking, but I don't believe in coincidence. As this thought struck me, I heard Antoine's voice begin to interact with mine, as is often the case when I am trying to work something out in my mind.

Antoine

You are wise when you say that you don't believe in coincidence Child. There is no such thing! Everything you do, and everything that happens is for a reason. There are no mistakes. Everything is perfect...everything is as it should be.

You Child, are experiencing a soul reconnection in a very personal way at this very moment in your physical life. You made the primary connection with your friend a very long time ago (as you understand time) when you first met each other in this incarnation. You and he both virtually incarnated at the same time, so you could meet and recognize each other early as part of the same Soul family. This was important, for without that you could not have found and recognized each other now. Many things had to be set in motion to allow that to happen.

Each aspect of your unique Blueprint, which you create before each incarnation has different strands of possibility attached to it. There is always one strand, or pathway that will lead to the highest possible outcome for your Soul growth. This Child, with your powers of discernment and intuition from a very young age is the one you chose to take. As the Teacher you have always been, you instinctively knew that to do that, you must turn your back, so to speak, on the other possibilities as they presented themselves to you throughout your life. This was one of those occasions.

One of the reasons that you chose your parents was because they had already agreed to relocate to that particular geographical location when you were a young child. This was an integral piece of your puzzle, but just one piece. There are still many more pieces to be experienced before your Blueprint is complete. At that particular time, the seeds were already sown for the spiritual path you had already chosen to take...the foundations were set. Many events were already set in motion to bring you to the exact point you have reached right now. Within that strand of possibility, you both had other important tasks to complete before this reconnection was scheduled to take place.

From a Human point of view, it would have been so much easier for you to have followed different strands on many occasions throughout your life. We know that there are some aspects of this lifetime that you have found difficult. We have seen this, and we have supported you, but with our encouragement, you did manage to write in a few rewards for your hard work along the way. This reconnection is one of them. You have agreed to interact in a way now that will be both helpful and beneficial to you both. You have kept to your script beautifully. This is your validation that you have arrived at this point right on schedule, and because you have, it naturally follows that so too has he.

We are so proud of you!

Well done Child!

Note: This reconnection has in fact, two sides to the story! Not only have I reconnected with an old school friend with whom I have much in common, but his wife understands who she truly is and has been following a spiritual path for many years now. She is in fact, a very knowledgeable and gifted Natural Healer. We complement each other on many levels, and we have been able to assist each other with our respective work in a very positive and profound way.

CHAPTER FIVE

I Am A Starchild...Understanding At Last

July 13th 2010

I had a very disturbed night last night with very little sleep. Most of the night was spent in a lucid dream state. I woke up every hour or two feeling extremely thirsty, and still experiencing the annoying headache I had gone to bed with. After drinking some water, I would doze off again, and then repeat the process, but the strange thing was that each time I did this, I would find myself right back where I was before. This did not feel like a dream; it felt more like I was out of body and actually experiencing another place, or another time. Dare I say that it may even have been another planet...one far more advanced than this one! The technology there was more advanced than ours, but there was a distinct feeling of oppression against the people. Everything appeared to be civilized, but there was an underlying fear...it was palpable! The people wore what we would consider to be space-age clothing.

I can't remember everything, but I do know that I

spent a lot of time running. I seemed to be involved in situations where some people in authority were chasing after a group of us. They appeared to know our whereabouts by using some sort of tracking device that alerted them with a beeping signal. They appeared instantaneously, and we had to run for our lives! I was really surprised when I thought about it afterwards because I always believed that civilizations as far advanced as this one would not practice oppression against the people. I have had similar experiences before, but on those occasions, the place I was experiencing was a much lesser developed place, or planet than our own. The people there virtually wore rags, and I felt that I was there in a helping capacity also.

When I finally dragged myself out of bed this morning, I was still feeling really exhausted, and I wondered what on earth was going on with me. I was tired all the time and not feeling well at all. I started to think about all the other things that were happening to me lately, and I also wondered if I might be going a bit crazy! Did I really believe that I was on another planet somewhere, helping with some sort of situation? I immediately heard Antoine telling me that I was not going crazy, and I was in fact, a *Starchild.* He said that was a part of the reason he called me *Child!* He sounded really elated, and I could sense a smile on his face. He said that he was really happy that I had finally woken up to who I was! I vaguely remembered a reference to Starchildren in a book I had read a few years ago, but I really had no idea what he was talking about. He told me to do some research, so that I might understand more fully.

I also remembered an out of body experience I had many years ago. It was in 1996, and I have it documented in my journal. I was asking for some guidance when I suddenly found myself in the company of a Being that called itself: *A representative of "The Friends to the Memorial of the Light Star."* It was a strange looking Being with long, slender, feminine arms, and hands with very sharp pointed fingernails. It was of a round shape with sharp spikes protruding from it everywhere, and I sensed that it could be very aggressive. I didn't feel comfortable in its presence at all! The conversation took place by mind transfer, and it demanded to know why I was there.

I told it who I was, and it asked me to wait. I looked down at the middle of the Being, and I saw a pulsating, pale red light about half way down its body. It said it had been given permission to communicate with me. I can't remember everything it said, but all of a sudden it became very aggressive towards me, and then yelled at me to "wake up!"

It said: *Wake up! Wake up to who you are!* Then it began to stick its long, sharp fingernails into me, and I experienced real pain...so much so that I couldn't stand it any longer, and I became frightened. I asked my Spirit Guides to please get me out of there, and then I immediately found myself back in my physical body. I was literally shaking, and I still remember the feeling it left me with all these years later. I feel that Spirit was trying to wake me up to my Truth way back then...to tell me who I truly was.

I entered the word *Starchild* into the computer, and I found one particular website that I felt really connected to. It presented me with a lot of information and understanding, especially about some of the physical symptoms I have been experiencing for some time. Parts of the puzzle were put in place for me, and I spent most of the day on it. In the evening, I decided to scroll through to see what else I could find, and I found another site that I immediately felt drawn to. It featured a C.D. with a beautiful ethereal image of a young child on the cover. There was a beautifully written quote underneath it.

When I saw the name of the author, I couldn't believe my eyes! What were the odds? It was Antoine! I felt him laughing, and I laughed with him; he has a wonderful sense of humor. All my doubts about everything were blown away in an instant. It was the validation I needed once and for all! I was so excited that I immediately rang one of my Daughters to share it with. She was blown away by it too! I will never doubt his presence again...he is very real to me, and he is leading me on a wonderful, exciting journey.

Thank you Antoine.

Note: This may be a different and perhaps a difficult concept for some of you to grasp, but it is my understanding that there may in fact be several aspects of the same Soul which incarnate at the same time. Not only are those aspects capable of incarnating in Human form, as we have chosen to do here on Planet Earth, but they may also choose to incarnate on other planets and in different dimensions of reality. This might be when our help is needed for some kind of evolutionary process that is taking place there, and this is always an act of Universal Service ...of Universal Love.

We have all lived in different realities and in different

planetary systems at different times, and I believe that it is quite possible for us to visit there while we are still in physical form in this reality...perhaps during sleep, either in a dream state of consciousness, or while operating out of body in our Light Body. Because we are simply different aspects of the same Soul...the same energy, I also believe that it is entirely possible for us to enter into and connect with that energy, and to actually experience the reality of those other aspects of our self...our Soul. We can then retain the memory of that experience as our own when we return to this reality because it is in fact, our memory!

We are all multidimensional, spiritual beings.

I believe that I am, simply put, a Child of the Stars.

I believe that we all are!

PART TWO

CHAPTER ONE

Finding Lightcrow

In keeping with my usual practice, I was speaking with Antoine one night just before sleep when I felt compelled to ask him if there might be others like him, who might want to communicate with me. He didn't answer me, but I could feel his energy shift, and then move aside to be replaced with a different one. This new, obviously male energy had a very intense and authoritative feel to it, and his voice was very deep. He sounded and felt very different to Antoine, whose energy is softer, and more gentle and peaceful.

I recognized this energy; I have felt this same energy before on very rare occasions. This has only been in recent years when I have been asking for guidance to assist some particular person along their spiritual path. Although I did not hear a voice as such, and he did not introduce himself to me at all, the first time I felt this energy, the name Lightcrow immediately came to me; however, I was never certain about it, and I thought perhaps I had just imagined it. I decided that I would simply refer to that particular energy by that name anyway!

This time there was no mistaking his name, or his words to me.

There was absolutely no doubt in my mind that this communication was real!

"I am Sage! I am as old as the Sun and the Moon and the Stars in the night sky, and I gaze upon you with loving eyes Dear One. I offer you words that are meant for all of Humanity.

I am of the Crow!

I am of the Light!

I am Lightcrow!

Hear our words. Hear our pleas. Feel the longing of our ancestors for the land to be returned to what they once knew. Feel the sadness, and know that we welcome you with our arms and our hearts open wide. We have waited! You have waited! Now it is time Dear One. Rest now and we will speak again. It will be easier for you now that the connection has been made. It was always meant to be this way.

Our heart is your heart.

Our Love is your Love.

Our wisdom is your wisdom.

It shall be done!

In 1998 I had a visitation from a male spirit entity, who told me that my help was needed.

I had just been diagnosed with thyroid cancer, and I was experiencing all the normal anxieties associated with that. I must be honest here, and admit to feeling some doubt in my mind as to whether I would make it through and survive. I am now sure this communication was to reassure me that I would be alright because I still had important work to do here!

Journal: April 1st 1998

I couldn't go back to sleep after waking during the night, so I snuggled into my husband's back for comfort. Almost immediately, I became aware of a man standing at the foot of my bed. Initially, I felt frightened and tried to shake my husband to tell him, before finally yelling at him. I soon realized that he couldn't hear me, or feel me because I was slightly out of body. The man moved around to the side of the bed closest to my husband, and he put his face up close to mine.

My fear dissolved when I realized that he was in spirit. He appeared to be in his thirties, and he had dark hair, a beard and a moustache. He told me that the Two Virgins of The Earth were dying, and I must help. I asked him why he was asking me because I had no idea what he was talking about...he should be talking to my husband, who might understand these things. He told me that he wasn't talking to him about it because he didn't have the wisdom for this task, but I did. I told him that I didn't understand, but he disappeared!

The next thing I knew, I was hearing a conversation between two men. I often hear conversations in the spirit world. This one was an in-depth conversation about the problems the Earth is experiencing today, and what we as Human Beings need to do about it. I understood what they were saying at the time, but I came back with little memory of it!

Note: I have since come to the understanding that he was referring to the two poles...the Arctic and the Antarctic as the Two Virgins of The Earth, and I now also believe that he may have been specifically talking about the shifting of the two poles that is taking place right now on our planet. He was telling me that Mother Earth herself was in crisis, and She needed my help in some way.

In 2008 I had a very moving, lucid dream. In fact, I

believed at the time, and I still do that it was a visitation because it was so real.

Journal: April 14th 2008

Lucid dream early this morning: My husband and I were outside our house, but it was a bit different to this one, and there appeared to be a lot of space around us. We were beside the side fence, looking at a magnificent rose growing over a wooden arbor. The rose was a whitish pink, and it was hanging right down to the ground. I told my husband that he would have to prune it back because as it was, there was no room to walk under it. I looked up, and suddenly realized that the rose was actually growing from the garden next door, and it was creeping over the fence and onto our arbor. I could see workmen working on the house next door; they seemed to be doing something to the roof. There were also men working with some bricks.

Suddenly, I heard a loud noise like the sound of horses galloping, and as I looked up towards the wide wire gate at our side entrance, I was amazed to see an American Indian riding a beautiful brown horse with white on its nose and feet. He had a single feather in his dark hair, which he wore in long plaits, and he was fairly young. He wore a beaded top that showed off a lot of his chest, and I noticed that he had long breeches covering his legs, and moccasins on his feet. He was smiling at me, and he was surrounded by what appeared to be a whole nation of Indians...they had their chests bare and only wore loin cloths and moccasins.

The people working next door all took fright and ran away, but I seemed to be overcome with excitement, and I ran to open the gate, so they could all come in. Some came through, and others went next door. I looked for the one with the feather...I felt that I knew him somehow. I saw him on the other side of the fence, looking at me through what appeared to be like a sheet of glass, or some sort of thin, transparent material. I felt very peaceful and much loved.

The next thing I remember, I was bringing a cup of tea out to my husband. We both sat on the verandah of an old brick house with beautiful views across some paddocks, and we both appeared to be very happy and contented.

Sachqua

Not long after the first channel from Lightcrow in 2010, I had a visit from a spirit entity, who introduced himself to me as Sachqua (or Saqua). He was the same one who appeared to me all those years ago and told me that the Two Virgins of The Earth were dying, and I must help. His dark features were exactly the same, but this time he wore the traditional clothing of the Eskimo, including the hooded, fur-trimmed, skin jacket.

I would have recognized him anywhere!

He told me that he is attached to the wolf Arkala and also to Lightcrow, as well as to me. He also told me that others like him will be coming through to me at different times. I am to be their voice to Humanity. Many are waiting for their words.

I have agreed to do this work with them.

I am ready!

CHAPTER TWO

Lightcrow

ather the people to you Dear One... I have much to say to them through you. There is much I need to tell them...much Truth I need to impart, for the time is upon us.

The time for the Truth to be told!

All beings are equal...none is more than the rest...all are part of the whole.

We have walked the Earth together you and I...when the night was clear and the stars were bright...when the Earth was clean and the air was pure. We were as one with Mother Earth and all her inhabitants. We relied on each other for sustenance, and our path was uncomplicated and clear. We were as one then, and it must be this way again! The many must change to join the few, so all will finally know and understand the Truth.

We lived off the land and all was provided. Everything the tribe needed was provided by Mother Earth and nothing was wasted. She must not be raped any longer; She is dying! *The Two Virgins of the Earth are dying;* She must be saved at all costs! Humanity must once again learn to live within her rising vibration if it is to survive as a species; otherwise, it will be cast away and shed from Her...just as a snake sheds its skin when it is no longer useful.

Many of you now are not even aware of what sustains you. Some are, but most are not. Most of you exist within the material world created by you. This is a wondrous thing, but not when it becomes your God and you forget who you truly are. You must wake up, all of you, and reconnect with the natural world around you. You must find ways to improve the sustainability of the Earth, if you are to continue to exist within Her sphere, but to do that, you must first become consciously aware of Her and Her great gift to you. Remove your blinders! You do not see! Most of you are so caught up in the lives you have created that you do not see what is around you...the beauty and the Love that exists, not just within nature, but within yourself. You have come to see yourself as separate, but you are not separate. You never have been and you never will be. You are as One with All That Is; you are a part of the whole. You must learn to tap into and connect with the hum of the universe once again...the All That Is.

What has happened? You were all aware of this once;

you were as one with nature; you knew no differently. You understood that death was not death; it was simply returning Home...to the hum. You are so afraid of death now; what for we ask you? It is as natural as your breath on the wind...as the water flowing through the Earth...as the stars in the night sky, and as the fire in your belly. Your animal species understands this; you understood this. What has happened? All the problems Humanity faces today: The wars; the hatred; the intolerance; the jealousy; the greed and the violence. All of these are fear based. What are you afraid of? There is no need to be afraid of anything; there is nothing that exists that you need to be afraid of!

You do not know who you are anymore; you feel lost! You are floundering around in the dark, moving this way and that way, looking for the light switch. You look everywhere outside yourself for this, but you will never find it there. You must look within yourself because it exists only within you.

You feel disconnected from the Light because you no longer recognize who you are. You are a part of nature...a part of the whole. You have to find your way back; you have to connect once again. You all must be lead to this understanding for Humanity to survive; you must understand this!

Remember *Dear One* when the plains were fertile with all manner of wildlife and plant life, and we lived in complete balance and harmony. All our needs were provided: Food; clothing; shelter and companionship. The wolves especially were our friends. I know that you remember this because Arkala is still with you, and I know that you see her often. She watches over you constantly with Love; she will allow no harm to come to you. She was your constant companion and protector then, and she continues to be now. She has intervened on many occasions to keep you safe because she is as one with you. She understands your connection, just as all your other animal companions understand, and there have been many of those!

Your governments; your financial institutions; your societal structures; all these have been created by Humanity and they are still operating within the older, denser vibrational energies that have previously existed on the Earth Plane. You think that you still need them, but you do not. They must fall! You must develop new ways of existing within the new, lighter, higher vibrational energies that are now washing onto your planet and into the consciousness of the new Human

Being. The old ways are not working any longer …you must see that! It confronts you daily on your television screens and in your personal lives…all the negative images and behaviors of many people who no longer fit into the moulds that man has created. This creates discord and disharmony. Man must learn to be responsible enough to govern himself!

This game you have created of Follow the Leader; it is finished! All of you are leaders, but you just don't remember this yet; some do, but most do not. You insist on giving your power away to others; you give it to cults and religions; to sports and so called celebrities; to the media; throughout all walks of life and in every manner of ways. It is time now to take back your power and to remember who you truly are. It is time to live within your Truth once again; time to live responsibly in balance and harmony once again.

Each of you holds a piece of the puzzle inside you; you simply have to find it. When all of the pieces are in place, the puzzle will be complete and The New World will emerge as if by magic. You all know how to do this; you just have to remember! Human Beings have always loved playing games. Think of your life with Mother Earth as one magnificent game you have created. You all know how to play this game well, or you would not be there at this critical time in your evolution. You have all chosen to be there. Just as you are waking up *Dear One,* so must the rest.

You do not need to be unconscious any longer to exist on the Earth plane. You can now consciously remember what you have forgotten.

It is time!

Many of us are helping you to do this in many different ways. We are reaching out to you from these planes of existence, and we are holding your hands with our hands and your hearts with our hearts.

We hope that you feel our Love and encouragement.

Indeed, that is our purpose!

CHAPTER THREE

Connecting With Nature

Greetings Dear Ones,

Many of you will say that you cannot leave your cities and your way of life, and you need what the cities provide to survive; you need your job; you need the conveniences and the shopping; you need your lifestyle, or you will not be happy; you need what you have created to be happy; however, some of you, in ever increasing numbers are doing just that. You are choosing something different, and in so doing, you are beginning to wake up and remember who you truly are.

We say to you: You can have both if that is your choice. You are not being asked to give up your lives; you are not being asked to give up your cities; you are simply being reminded that you may need to make changes to the way you live, in order to bring your lives back into balance and harmony.

Nature is all around you, even in the largest and busiest of cities, but do you see it?

Are most of you even aware of it?

Turn off your television sets and your entertainment devices, and turn off your night lights. If enough of you do this, you will be able to view and connect to the wonders of the night sky. What better way to connect to the hum and the perfection of the universe? You cannot do this now because of the profusion of artificial light in your cities. Is it really all necessary? The magic is there, but many of you just can't see it! Most of you don't even bother to look at it except in passing. How long is it since you have experienced the wonders of a clear night sky? How long is it since you have watched the sun rise and set? How long is it since you have immersed yourself in the magic of a full moon? You will say that you don't have time in the busy lives you have created to be a part of your natural world, but this is necessary if you are to wake up! You must make time! Your man made devices alone will not sustain your spirit, but you manage to make time for those!

Play in your parks and admire your beautiful gardens; eat freshly grown produce; engage with the animal kingdom; walk in your forests; swim in your streams and oceans, and feel the sand between your toes; connect with, and be at one with the natural world around you; feel yourself as part of it. All these things will sustain your spirit and your physical body; indeed, all these things will help you to wake up.

They will all remind you of who you truly are.

They are all reflections of Home...your true Home.

Do these things consciously and in a state of awareness, and your vibrational frequency can't help but rise. You will begin to wake up as surely as your sun will rise and set!

As you set these things in motion, you will feel your heart center shift and begin to open. As you feel the connection take place, you will begin to feel Love for all of creation, including each other because you will no longer feel separate. You will feel a part of the whole; you will feel complete. Your perceived need for material creations will fall away, and eventually so too will greed and jealousy and intolerance. All the things that are fear based; all the negative energies that influence your societies at this time will magically fall away.

Let these things fall away.

They serve you no longer!

You are becoming lighter. Your Light Body is expanding as you become fully conscious, and more of your physical body is filling with this new higher, lighter vibrational energy, and this new energy is simply Love!

When Man can Love himself as well as each other without fear, there will be no need for leaders. You will be responsible enough to lead yourself, and there will be no crime and no hurting or killing each other because this lower vibrational energy will no longer be a part of your collective consciousness; it will simply not exist!

After this first channel, I spoke with my spirit guide - Antoine.

Me: Antoine, I am feeling a little overwhelmed by all this.

Antoine: You need not be Child. You are well and truly up to the task at hand. As you already understand, Didi and I are always with you on a personal level. Lightcrow is a Master Teaching Guide, and you and he have lived and worked together before. There could be no better team for this work. If only you could remember who you truly are on this side of the veil, you would understand, but you have asked us to keep this information from you while you are in a conscious state. We intend to honor your request, but know that you are much revered here, and we honor you and the work we do together.

Journal: September 14th 1997

I was having an afternoon nap when I suddenly found myself outside my physical body. I was outside the house looking through the wide glass doors into the kitchen area when I noticed something moving inside. As I watched, a beautiful big wolf sauntered over to the door and looked straight out at me. She had her head down, but her eyes were looking directly into mine. They were a beautiful vivid blue-green color, and her fur was a gorgeous light color with darker colors around the edge of her ruff. I immediately recognized her as being like the wolf my husband has spoken of seeing in his meditations. In his meditations, he is often greeted by an Indian Chief and a wolf; although, I feel by her reaction to me that this one is connected to me.

Note: Since the time of this meeting with her, I am able to simply close my eyes and ask for her. I concentrate, and she appears to me through my third eye vision. She is always in black and white, and her eyes are always shining with a soft golden light. It is like viewing the negative image of a photograph. The first time she came to me this way, I asked her name and the name *Arkala* flashed immediately into my mind. I did some research and to my surprise, I found out that the name *Arkala* simply means: *She Wolf.*

While relaxing down and preparing to channel, I was feeling frustrated by all the distractions of my daily life. I was trying to write down the teachings from Lightcrow as he was speaking, and I was constantly being distracted with pets etc. Suddenly, I received a vision through my third eye area, which showed him with his lips moving. At first, I thought that he was trying to tell me that I would be able to focus more clearly if I was able to see this vision, but I suddenly felt compelled to use my tape recorder. I began to repeat his words into the recorder as he spoke, and then I simply transcribed them later.

The following is the first channel using this new process, and it is clearly meant specifically as encouragement to me.

Lightcrow
Greetings Dear One,

I come to you once again with Love in my heart and gratitude for the work you do with us. Don't worry so

Dear One, the connection between us will become clearer as we go along. Perhaps you need to move into a more peaceful space for this work where there can be no distractions for you. You will then be able to focus on my words.

We have played together you and me. Can you feel the wind in your hair? We have hunted together you and me. We were brothers. Can you feel the earth between your hands? Can you feel the water beneath your feet? Can you feel the sun upon your face? Remember these things!

They are who we were.

They are who we are.

Do you remember when the white man came and disturbed our peace? We wished him no harm; we understood that all men are one; indeed, all creatures are one. He was afraid of us, so he made us his enemy. He threatened our women and our children and our way of life. We had no choice but to fight back; to fight for the good; to fight for the Light. That time is past! There is no need to fight now; there is no threat. The only threat is perceived in the mind of the perpetrator. It is time now to put down the weapons and to stop the destruction. It is time now to build a new world...one where there is no place for anger and hatred...one where man will help each other.

This is the only way to go.

This is the only way to grow.

See me on the hill **Dear One,** sitting proud upon my stallion. Remember that vision!

Remember who I am!

Remember who you are!

The time has come once again for you to speak your Truth...to stand proud and to sit tall upon your stallion on that hill. Take your place beside me now, and we will ride together as brothers.

The brothers we have always been.

The brothers we will always be.

CHAPTER FOUR

Connecting With Each Other

The following channel came through very clearly early one morning; I was half asleep and not expecting it. I knew that it was Lightcrow because I recognized his energy, but the timbre of his voice had changed slightly. It was deeper than before, and he sounded as though he was talking underwater...a bit like Darth Vader! Perhaps I was so sleepy that I didn't have the channel entirely open, but I had no difficulty understanding him; in fact, I understood him very easily.

Lightcrow

Greetings Dear Ones,

We come to you once again with Love in our hearts. You have had a popular saying in your world for some time: *Think outside the square.* Our saying would be: *Think outside the box* because you have been operating within a third dimensional reality until now. Many of you have been doing this, and very well we might say. Now we ask you: *Step outside the box,* and into a new reality...fearlessly and with courage, and find more of the magic awaiting you there.

This is the only way to go.

This is the only way to grow!

As your energy rises in vibration, you will be able to extend it further and further. As your light shines with this new energy, people will be drawn to you like moths to a flame. It is time now to connect with each other in a new way. Some of you are already doing this, in many different ways and on many different levels, but there is much more work to be done for most of you. Don't be afraid to show your Light, for many are searching for it, and you will be drawn together as your light extends. More and more people will be drawn into this web of attraction. They are all searching, but many do not know what they are searching for. When they find it, and when they feel it, they will instinctively recognize this Light within themselves also.

They will begin to wake up as if from a long slumber, and they will begin to remember who they truly are... spiritual creator beings of energy and Light, who have chosen to inhabit a Human body, in order to experience the world of matter. This is what you have forgotten; this is the ultimate Truth; this is true for all sentient beings on your planet!

Many of you are reaching out through the Ethernet. You have created incredible social networks with your many devices. This is indeed wondrous! You are learning to tap into the hum of the universe. Everything in your world; indeed, everything in your universe is comprised of this same Ether. By utilizing this medium, you can reach out to many, and you can connect in whichever way you feel comfortable. Your younger ones know and understand this. They instinctively know how to connect this way, and they do so naturally and without fear. Nothing is hidden; they say what is in their hearts because their heart centers are open wide. They speak their Truth and they hide nothing and share everything. They don't keep their feelings hidden inside with shame and fear like your older ones were taught to do. That time has now finished!

There is no place in the New World for this way of thinking. Your older generations are now starting to learn to do this also. You must all learn to do this, and eventually allow the old way of thinking to fall away; it serves you no longer.

Do not be afraid; there is nothing to fear!

Everything that was hidden is now being revealed.

This will become more so as your energies shift, and your heart centers open wider and wider. There will be no more secrets. The lies woven throughout the fabric of your history are now being detected and revealed on a larger scale than ever before. This is now beginning to happen on all levels of your societies; you are witnessing it on a global scale at this very moment. As you begin to understand and feel comfortable with this concept, more and more of you will begin to connect with your hearts open wide, and without judgment.

At this point in your evolvement, you still need your electronic devices to connect in this way, but we say to you: The time will come when you will not need those devices. You have the potential to use your Human brain as a computer, and it is the most advanced computer of all. You will learn to tap into the universal energies very easily. There are a few of you, who have developed this ability already, but very few. The new Human will be able to see and feel everything. Lies will be easily detected, and you will no longer be able to deceive each other. This old way of being will not be supported by the new energies, and will simply fall away and magically disappear. As your energy fields expand, they will begin to push against each other and overlap, and you will begin to feel each other in a new and different way.

You will begin to feel compassion for your fellow man. You will begin to understand that you are not different; indeed, you are all the same. You will begin to understand that you all laugh and cry and Love in the same way. When you feel each other in this way, you will understand that you are all one; you will understand that there is no need to fear each other because you are not separate. You will finally understand that you can allow yourselves to Love and support each other.

Although there is much work you have undertaken at this time, we want you to understand that you are also meant to enjoy your physical life. Our wish for you is that you will play often together, and have a happy, joyous and fun filled experience. The more you reach out to each other, and the more you extend your energy field and raise your vibration, the more people you will be able to reach; the more people you will be able to extend a helping hand.

Your younger ones have come to break down the barriers; indeed, to show you the new way. They have much to teach you. You may not see it this way, but it is so! Watch them and listen to them, for they have much to tell you; they have much to show you. They bring the new energy through with them. Many of them feel displaced and disoriented on your planet where the old energy is still operating on many levels. This is often evident in their behavior. They have displayed great courage in choosing this work, but they know on a Soul level the important role they will play; not only now, but into your future. They do not feel balanced or in harmony with the older, heavier energies; they don't understand them. They only feel balanced and comfortable with the new energy that is emerging throughout your world. They will show you the way!

You all have great courage.

We from these planes of existence applaud you!

Note: For a number of years now, there have been waves of Human Beings incarnating on our planet, who operate within a higher level of consciousness than we have been used to in the past. This first started happening during the 1970`s. This first wave is referred to as *The Indigo Children* because that is the main color they exhibit within their aura. They came first to kick-start the changes that must occur within our societies, and to pave the way for *The Crystal Children,* who began to make their appearance around the beginning of the new millennium. Apparently these children will be the ones making the greatest contribution to the connection process.

These special children exhibit the golden rays in their aura, and are extremely psychic. They are able to "read" people to the extent that they know when they are being lied to, and they have no inhibitions about exposing those lies! They seem to have such a high vibrational energy level that it can be hard work sometimes simply to have them in your space. Anyone who has had anything to do with these children will know exactly what I am talking about!

I also have the ability to know when I am being lied to, and I can tell you that it can be extremely disconcerting at times, especially when Loved Ones are involved!

There are a number of excellent books and websites dedicated to these special "New Kids on the Block," and you will have access to much more information on this subject from those sources if you choose to.

There are also many Souls...a large number of these incarnated again fairly soon after the end of the Second World War, who have agreed to raise their consciousness at this time in Human evolution to help Humanity understand the many changes that are taking place in our societies. Many of these people have come as Teachers and Healers. These changes have to take place for Humanity to survive. We cannot keep treating Mother Earth or each other in the way that we have done in the past. She will not support us if we do; She will simply evolve without us!

I believe that I am one of these Souls.

I also believe that if you are reading these words, it is very likely that so too are you!

CHAPTER FIVE

Taking Back Your Power And Responsibility

Greetings Dear Ones,

We see you there, standing at the foot of the precipice, looking up with excitement building, preparing to ascend...just like children off on some long awaited journey. We feel your excitement, and we hope that you feel our Love and encouragement.

To many, it may appear that the task you have undertaken is somewhat daunting, but we say to you that it need not be such hard work. The only rule of spiritual ascension is that there are no rules! You are the Creators, and you will ascend in your own way and in your own time, but you are now being pushed forward at a faster pace on new waves of energy, and this shift in consciousness will take place much faster than you could have ever imagined. One thing you will all begin to understand is that you must take back your own power, and you must also take responsibility for yourself and for your own actions. Ideally, this will be done in a responsible manner, and in a way that has the needs of all mankind at its heart. As you reach this place of responsibility, you will begin to understand that the way you have done things in the past is not the way forward; that time is now finished.

Some of you will instinctively embrace the new ways, but many of you will find it difficult to let go of your Truth as you have understood it until now. We say to you: Truth is not static; it is forever evolving...just as you are, and it is different for each of you. What you have understood as your Truth yesterday may not necessarily be the same as it will be for you today, or tomorrow. You have created many attachments to your Human way of thinking, especially those within your religious belief systems. Until now, Human Beings have operated within the denser energy fields that have previously affected your planet. You have operated within the concept of duality; such as good and evil, or right and wrong. Judgment is a Human condition, and it has served you in the past, but it will not be supported by the new energies that are now washing onto your planet, and into your new way of thinking. You will begin to use discernment in all that you say and do, rather than make judgments as you have done previously.

Many concepts you may have judged as wrong in the

past will eventually be revealed to you as a new Truth, and many of you will not know what to do with this. We know that change is difficult for most of you to accept, especially when there is such a large leap of consciousness as at this time. There will be those who will be determined to swim against the current, and they will be very loud and disruptive in their protests. These will go down kicking and screaming, so to speak! Once they realize that they are unable to stop the tide of new energy from coming in, and these changes are a natural part of which they are becoming, they will begin to accept the transformation process within themselves; they will begin to accept their new Truth.

Although initially based in Truth, the majority of your religious teachings have undergone much Human intervention throughout your history of time. The teachings have at times been deliberately "colored" by your so called men of knowledge and authority, and the intended meanings of these teachings will now be revealed and understood in the way that they were originally given. Why has this been you ask? It was simply done to keep the enormity of your power hidden from you. That way they could exercise their power of control over you. If you had understood who you truly were, you would have been seen as a threat to their perceived authority. Some of you knew, and you spoke up and even practised your Truth, but you were cruelly persecuted for your beliefs; many still are! It is only when you all understand that you are all a part of God, indeed, all a part of the One, and you are all Creators that peace will reign on your planet.

Only when the layers of authority and deceit within these structures have been peeled away will the higher Truth be revealed. Your power will be reclaimed by each and every one of you. This is already beginning to happen because you are revealing this Truth to yourself. You are asking the questions, and you are receiving the answers from that vast part of yourself which remains connected to the Source. You will regain your power because that power is simply your understanding of the higher Truth. You will not be deceived any longer, and you will no longer want to give your power away. This is the natural way of things, and it is just simply the way it must be.

There are many people already in place within your Governments and Financial Institutions, and all the other places you perceive as having authority within your societies. These people are waking up at an ever faster rate. They are the ones who will step forward with courage and begin to make the necessary changes. This is already beginning to happen. As your time progresses, there will be many younger ones riding the new energy waves, and they will take their place beside and behind them. They have brought the new ways with them; they know exactly why they are there, and they will instinctively know how to implement the necessary changes. There will be no room for doubt or uncertainty.

It will simply be done!

They will have an innate understanding of what is responsible, and that understanding will reflect the needs of the New Human and the New Earth; they have the answers! There will be no leaders amongst them because they understand that they are all leaders, and they will all take responsibility for their own actions; they will simply know no other way. This shift will take place on a mass scale. The older ones will lead the charge, and the younger ones will follow through and complete the process.

As with any ascension into a higher altitude, many of you may suffer with some degree of altitude sickness, which will be reflected within your physical bodies. For most this will be mild, and for some more troublesome, but we can assure you that it will always only be temporary. There are simple measures you can take to help alleviate these symptoms. Please make sure that your nutritional needs and water requirements are adequately met, and please continue to exercise regularly. You will also need to keep yourself well grounded by continuing to remain present in your everyday activities. This is important! You will especially need to maintain your connection with your natural world and with each other.

As you make the climb, your physical body will come into alignment with the newer, higher, lighter energies, and as it adjusts, the symptoms will disappear. They will fall away…just as your old way of thinking will fall away. You will expand on this new way of thinking, and you will begin to see everything around you in the new light of understanding.

You will begin to feel the energy of your own power returning. For too long it has been in the keeping of others, who have often not used it with integrity. Many of them have used it to their own advantage with greed at the core of their intention. This will no longer be tolerated by you!

Why has the power been held by so few in the past you

ask? This has simply been the way of your existence within the older energies on your planet. You were so eager to give your power away because if you didn't own it, then you didn't have to take responsibility for it.

On a conscious level, most of you didn't even realize that you possessed this power. You always believed that you were separate and perhaps inferior to those you perceived as holding authority. It was easier for you that way, and there were always those ready to take that power and abuse it. But as you become conscious of owning it once again, you will begin to see that you are all in authority; indeed, you always have been.

None is more or less than the rest.

You are ready, and so the takeover begins!

We watch with great interest and anticipation, and we applaud you all!

Note: For some time now, I have been plagued with a number of physical symptoms, which have become so annoying and troublesome that I have finally sought a medical opinion; however, no medical explanation can be given for most of them. Sinusitis and allergies, as well as disturbed sleep patterns have taken their toll on me, but by far the worst has been the ongoing problems that I have been experiencing with heart rhythm and palpitations.

This makes perfect sense to me when I think about it because if our vibrational energy is rising, our hearts will need to make the necessary adjustments to the rhythm, in order to accommodate that; however, I think that it is relevant to state here that if you are experiencing anything like this, it is important not to just assume that this is the reason for it.

It is of the utmost importance that it be properly investigated first.

CHAPTER SIX

A New Beginning...A Time for Change

January 1st 2011

Greetings Dear Ones,

We have witnessed many of you celebrating your festive season once again, and we see the joy these celebrations bring to you. We hope that even with all the changes occurring within your world right now and into your future that you will choose to continue to practice these important traditions with your families and friends...the joining of hands and hearts, and the joining as one, but perhaps with a new level of understanding; perhaps with an understanding of the true meaning of these special celebrations...the connection of the entire Human family.

Can you continue to ignore the fact that not everyone on your planet is treated equally, and that not everyone's needs are met? You have not yet learned that all of mankind is your family; all of the animal kingdom is your family; all that exists on, and within your planet is your family; indeed, all that exists within your universe is your family.

You have attached so much of what you have created on the material plane to your special gatherings that much of the real meaning has been lost, especially for your younger ones. We draw close to you at these special times and we see what takes place, and what is truly in your hearts. You are now heralding in a new year...a new beginning. The meaning of this is more profound than you can possibly realize at this time. This will be a time of great change upon your planet. These changes will start on a small scale, but they will gather momentum until a new understanding of connection filters through and into your societies, in a way that will reach into the hearts of everyone.

You have already created enough material goods to last you many lifetimes, but still you create more! These many baubles and pretty things that you term your possessions; do they make you feel as happy and as satisfied as they once did, or do you feel as though there is something missing now? Look deeply within yourselves to answer this question truthfully; you might be surprised with your answer. We would not be surprised to learn that many of you feel that there is something missing now because the shift is already taking place within you.

Why do the few have so much and the many have so little when the universe is capable of providing abundance for all? Are you so afraid of lack that you have overcompensated? This cannot happen if you exist within a place of balance and harmony.

You have forgotten that to create this place of balance, all energy must keep flowing freely and be distributed evenly; otherwise, it will become blocked. Why do many of you accumulate so much of what you term "possessions?" Could it be that you have forgotten that you don't "own" any of it, and it is all just an illusion created by you? Or is it simply greed and self-service?

We simply ask you to start changing your perception now and know that everything your physical body and your spirit needs is already provided by the universe...the Source...the All That Is.

How do I do this you ask? The answer is quite simple: As your physical body changes and your vibration rises, so too will your point of perspective; it will happen quite naturally. While you have been operating within the third dimensional reality, you have only been able to see so far behind and in front of you before your vision has become blocked. This is much like encountering the horizon and not being able to see beyond it, but as your consciousness rises and it begins to align with the higher dimensions, your point of perspective will also rise.

Because you will be observing everything from a higher vantage point, you will be able to see a lot further in all directions. As this happens, one of the outcomes will be that you will find that your desire for physical "attachments" will begin to fall away. You simply won't feel the need for them any longer; indeed, some aspects of your life that you previously considered important will no longer be of such relevance to you.

With this shift in consciousness and with your new perception, many of your belief systems will "crash." We want you to be consciously aware of this now, and to understand why this is happening. The tide is turning on your planet, and as with any turn of tide there will be a backwash. This is what many of you are experiencing at this very moment. All the old ways are being collectively washed back into the ocean…the Ether; cleared out if you like, to make way for new ways of thinking and of being. We know many of you will be feeling this as a loss, but we say to you: This feeling will only be temporary. You will all eventually embrace this new way of being; you will know no other way. You are creating something new and magical!

Meditation will help you greatly at this time; whichever way works best for you. There is no right or wrong way...only different ways. These practices will help to facilitate the opening of your heart centre, and this will allow the new energies to flow smoothly through you and out into your world, helping to create your new reality.

This clearing out of the old is not just happening within you, but within Mother Earth as well. She is cleansing herself by releasing all of her old energy patterns, in order to bring in the new. She is purging Herself of all the negativity she has carried for you as the Human species for so long and rejuvenating Herself with the new lighter, higher energies that She now has access to. You will witness this on many levels. Some you will judge as negative and destructive, but this is important and necessary work. This is beginning to happen on a physical level right now. Your weather patterns are changing, and they may appear to you as chaotic and disruptive, but we say to you: There is order within that perceived chaos. All birthing is painful, and this is what She is doing now; She is presenting you with a wonderful gift...a new life; indeed, the ability to continue to live within her vibration as the New Human Being with a higher level of consciousness than ever before.

She is helping you to create your New World.

Our wish for you as you welcome in your New Year would be that you can all roll as comfortably and as easily as possible in with the new waves as they crash upon your shore, and we say to you: *Please take the time to enjoy the ride!*

We are surfing the waves with you with Love in our hearts for each and every one of you.

We wish you well!

CHAPTER SEVEN

Wednesday January 11TH 2011

Lightcrow brought this communication through to me very early this morning. As I write this, we in Australia are witnessing some of the worst flooding in our living history; this is on a large scale. It is affecting most of our state of Queensland where I lived for most of my life. There is destruction on a mass scale with confirmed deaths, and a large number of people are missing; these are also expected to be fatalities. I have a personal connection to some of the worst hit areas with my younger Daughter and her fiancé still living in Toowoomba. Thankfully, they are safe! She listened to her intuition on the day of the flash flooding and decided not to go to work. If she had done so, she would have been right in the midst of the worst of it.; however, I have been concerned for her on a different level.

Her work within the local council there brings her into close contact with the media and the people directly affected by this disaster. She is a very empathetic person and is also very sensitive to the plight of people in distress, but even more so with the plight of our animal species. I knew that she would be feeling this sadness on a deep level. I can't even begin to imagine how many lives have been lost within our beloved animal kingdom.

For days now, I have had an uneasy feeling in the pit of my stomach that has been causing me to feel quite ill. I have been unable to work out why this was happening. I still feel this way, but at least now I understand what is affecting me. I am also feeling the sadness and the fear that is emanating from these areas; it is palpable to me! I am feeling the shock and the outpouring of loss and grief as if it was my own. This is not totally new for me, but I have never before experienced this in such a profound way.

I had reason to visit my Doctor yesterday, and while enduring a long wait, I experienced something else that was new for me. I have always been able to "read" people to a certain extent and know who they are on a Soul level, but this experience went further than that. There was a woman in the waiting room, and she was very obviously experiencing great discomfort; she was also very loud! I actually felt this person emotionally. I felt and understood that she had chosen to be ill, and to be in the pain she was so obviously experiencing. She had entered so far into her drama of needing attention that she had manifested her illness and her pain, in order to facilitate this.

The following channel was given to me for my personal understanding of what is occurring at the moment, but Lightcrow has made it clear to me that I am to include it in my writing for the benefit of everyone.

Lightcrow

We feel your anguish *Dear One,* and we draw close to you to bring words of comfort at this time.

Your loved one...the one you know in this lifetime as your younger Child is indeed much more than that. She is in fact, an old and very wise Soul; she has also answered the call to be of service to your planet at this critical time in your Human evolution.

She, like you has agreed to be a Support Worker for Humanity during this shift in consciousness, which is taking place right now. Also, as you know, she is a teacher, not just on a physical level, but also on a spiritual level. Because of this, she has the ability to help on both these levels. At this very moment in your time, she is exactly where she has chosen to be. She will bring much help and comfort, and a measure of understanding for the many people who will see themselves as the victims within this situation. She will also be able to provide the much needed practical help.

Many are in shock and frightened, and some will not recover from this. They did not believe these events possible, and they cannot make sense of what has happened to them and their communities. Many will now find themselves being drawn together within the common thread of loss and grief, to connect with and feel each other in a way that would not have been possible before. These, and also to some extent the ones who have experienced, or witnessed this event in a lesser way will begin to question. In so doing, they will begin to wake up.

They will begin to understand that there is much more to their physical lives than material possessions. They will begin to understand that the sense of security they felt with "owning" these things was all an illusion. They will start to realize that what is important in their lives is each other; in other words, they will begin to connect with each other. Every material thing you think you own can be gone from your reality in the blink of an eye. The Love and nurturing of each other; this is what is important in your Human lives; this can never be taken away from you, or ever lost to you.

Mother Earth is cleansing herself, and what you would term natural disasters is a part of this process. She is working in partnership with her own spiritual helpers. These you call the Nature Spirits, and they are working with you in a process of co-creation, in order to bring your world back into balance. This is what must happen for you to continue to exist within Her sphere. Some of you, for your own reasons have chosen not to remain there during this shift, and you have agreed to return Home as part of this cleansing process. We want you to understand that when this happens, it is always your choice; it is always a part of your contract. Through this sacrifice, if you choose to see it as such in your Human terms, much good comes.

We would simply remind you that these Loved Ones are never lost to you. No Human Being and no animal are ever lost. They have simply returned Home before you. They will be waiting here with us with loving hearts, to greet you and welcome you Home when it is your time to return. These are the sacrifices many of you have chosen to make to help bring your planet back into a place of peace and harmony, so that Humanity can continue to experience life within Her sphere.

Your Loved One will find a way to transmute her

feelings of sadness and distress at the huge loss of animal life. She will do this in a practical way that will help the animal survivors of this tragedy; she knows that she is there to help. She understands what is happening, and the important role she has chosen to play during this process.

You are changing at an accelerated rate now *Dear One,* and you are becoming more of your Light Body. This is why you are feeling people in this new way. You will become accustomed to this, and you will learn to embrace it because it is your natural state of being. We are here to help you; we would ask you to release your pain to us, and we will transmute that energy and return it to you as Love.

Feel our Love!

Breathe our Love Dear One!

I know Nature Spirits do exist because I met one fairly recently.

Journal: April 9th 2010

I was thinking how terrible it must be for the animals in cold climates through the winter months, and how many of them must suffer. This has concerned me ever since I made the move to Tasmania. Suddenly, the thought occurred to me that they must survive; otherwise, the different species would not survive.

I was immediately answered by a voice introducing itself to me as Eildie. I had the sense of a distinct female energy. She said that she was a Nature Spirit and she belonged to the forests and the mountains around where I live. She told me that these forests and mountains afford food and shelter for all animal life, even during the harshest of winters, and the nature spirits watched over them. She also told me not to worry so much about them because even Humans would never find these sanctuaries!

CHAPTER EIGHT

Moving Forward...Changing Relationships

We greet you once again Dear Ones,

We say to you: Within all the changes occurring in your Human lives at this time, one of the hardest for you to understand and accept will be the shifts in your relationships.

We want you to understand that as you move forward on this journey, there will be those around you who are not yet ready to make this climb with you. You might have to make the decision to leave them behind at some point along your path.

Letting go of friendships and other Human relationships does not necessarily mean letting go of the person, it simply means letting go of the attachments surrounding that person. You may still want these people in your life in some way, or perhaps you may not, but you will certainly not be as drawn into their everyday dramas and judgments as you once were. You will have moved beyond that way of thinking and you will simply no longer be in tune with it.

Because of this, you might not feel as attracted to the connection you share with them as you once were; you might feel more detached because you will be looking at them from your higher vantage point...your new, higher perspective. The things you both deemed important; indeed, those common threads that may have initially brought you together might no longer be felt by either of you. You will find that you will not form any judgment about this; you will simply accept it as your new Truth.

Some of these relationships may have been very important to you, and you will feel this loss in a profound way. We say to you that this is the natural way of things. Please do not be afraid to let go of these attachments. It simply means that you are moving on to something more in tune with your higher vibrational energy...your Higher Self, and in so doing; you are allowing the ones you have left behind to remain where they feel most comfortable at this time.

There will be others attracted to your Light, and they will move into your energy field, and into your new life and your new reality. You need never feel afraid of being alone, and you will find much more substance within these new relationships. Some of these may in fact be old connections you thought you had left behind, but these people might have actually been keeping pace with you, and they have simply caught up with you on the home stretch; they have agreed to meet you at some critical point along the way. You will be able to reach down and help them up onto the next foothold on the cliff face, and you can happily continue your journey together.

They too will be able to see what is ahead!

We say to you: Please, try not to be overly concerned about the ones you may feel the need to leave behind. All must make this same journey, and they will make it in their own time and in their own way. Eventually, you will all be at the same place together again; they will not be lost to you.

Their reasons for not moving forward with you at this time are theirs alone...only their Soul holds that knowledge. You cannot make their journey for them, but you can be there ready to assist them when they are ready to move forward and understand who they truly are.

There are many ways to make this transition. We would ask you not to try to force, or push others into moving with you. We would ask instead that you simply try to create a space in which you can allow your Truth to be known. If they recognize it as their own Truth, they will want to move with you; if not, do not close the connection completely, but instead we would ask that you simply move gently and lovingly away from the situation. The most loving thing you can do for them is to leave them behind because that is their choice, and that is what they need at this time. Continue moving forward yourself, and know that this has been your choice, and this is what you need at this time.

These shifts in relationships will apply to many aspects of your life, not just to Human relationships. As your energy shifts, you might find that your taste in music also changes. This is because you will be resonating with a different vibration. Your vibration will be attracted to the sound frequencies, or harmonics that are more in tune with that which you are becoming.

Your relationship with food might also change, especially when you begin to realize that you no longer want to sacrifice the lives of your precious animal family; when you begin to understand that they are no different to you, and they have a Soul just like you. You will also begin to listen to your own body when it tells you what you need to eat. You will begin to realize that Mother Earth has already provided everything you need for your optimum health.

In so doing, your relationship with your health will

also change. You will concentrate on preventative measures, rather than waiting until your physical body is ill before seeking help. This help will be freely available and will take many forms, but all will emanate from the knowledge that all illness is held in the etheric bodies first; those layers within the light body that hold all Human thought and emotion, before manifesting in the physical body. The negative emotional energies held there must be cleared out and returned to the ether to be transmuted, and balance restored; otherwise, you will literally make yourself sick!

Your relationship with money will also change, along with a myriad of different aspects within your life; all these will change. You will find that as you move further and further forward, you will be looking back at more and more, and you will eventually realize that your old life has been left behind; indeed, your old way of thinking has been left behind. You will have finally reached the summit! We say to you now that this achievement will not be the end of your journey, for in many ways, it will be just the beginning!

We want you to be prepared for these changes.

Embrace the new Dear Ones, just as we embrace you, and feel our Love and encouragement supporting you during your climb.

We Love you all!

CHAPTER NINE

For The Healers And The Teachers

Dear Ones,

We say to you now: You are all helpers on your planet at this time. Each of you holds a specific vibration within your Light Body to help make this shift in Human consciousness possible, but many of you do not remember this yet. We would simply ask that you begin to consciously remember this now.

To whom you term the Lightworkers of your planet... those who have already awakened, or are in the process of awakening, we would say to you now: Many of you are the Healers and the Teachers of your planet, and we specifically offer these words of Love and encouragement to you.

We can tell you now that each of you holds the energy of *The Ancient Ones* within your Light Body. This work is not new for you; indeed, you have done this same work before on your planet. Some of you may even have some memory of this; if not in your conscious state, perhaps in your dream state memory...that vast ocean of consciousness that holds the history of your many incarnations.

Much sadness and confusion prevails on your planet at this time, and the majority of Human consciousness does not comprehend what is taking place. The very fabric of Human life as you have known it is being ripped apart, and many have little true understanding of why this is happening. Most still see themselves as the flotsam and jetsam from the shipwreck being tossed around in the ocean at will by the natural currents, but you know this is not the Truth of it! There is order and purpose in everything.

The task you have undertaken as the Healers and the Teachers is to create the space to bring some measure of understanding and therefore healing into this situation for the rest of Humanity, and in so doing to help facilitate their awakening. We ask you to shine your Light as never before. This will not be an easy task for any of you, but we can assure you that you do know how to do this. Even though it is the most important of work, we would also ask that you spread this Light of understanding and healing in a very Human and playful way. Fun and laughter are wonderful Human attributes, and they are important vibrational factors in the healing of mind and body.

The teaching vibration is best felt by example. You do this well because it is a part of who you truly are. Live your life within your Truth; simply create the space to speak your Truth, and allow the Light of Love to shine from your heart into another. Always remember to lend a hand in practical ways whenever appropriate, but also remember that some will not want your help...in any form, and that is always their choice.

We would simply ask you to respect that choice.

Play often together. We love to watch you play together. It brings us great joy!

You chose to join the army of Lightworkers who incarnated on your planet at this critical time, in answer to the call for help from Mother Earth.

You are now being called into active duty.

You have chosen the path of service to Humanity, and you will be needed in an ever increasing way. As the shift accelerates, there will be many who would seek your counsel.

We are many, who are working with you and helping you from this side of the veil, and we would remind you that the veil grows thinner and weaker every day. Many more of you will now be catching glimpses of us in the shadows. You may even feel and hear our presence. We try to leave you little clues, and we give you signs that we are around you. An ever increasing number of you now know how to read these signs, and you are letting us know that you "get it!"

We love it when you do that!

We are always with you Dear Ones…never doubt us!

Note: Personally, I am seeing much more through the veil while I am in a conscious state than ever before.

Just recently, I was lounging sideways on my couch in the living room with my computer on my lap, totally immersed in my writing when I became aware of movement near the doorway into the hall. As I glanced towards it to see what it was, I was amazed to bear witness to a light grey cloud of mist heading towards the wall at the side of me; this is the wall between my living room and my guest bedroom at the back of the house. As I watched, it gathered speed, and then it seemed to condense and form a swirling vortex right next to my head. It disappeared with a loud whooshing sound… straight through the wall!

It all happened very quickly. I was so mesmerized that I didn't even move or speak until my husband, who had been sitting in a chair near me engrossed in the television asked me what on earth that loud whooshing sound was! He had heard it over the noise of the television, but hadn't seen it.

I know from personal experience that it is quite possible, in fact quite natural, to pass through walls and other solid objects, or what we perceive as being solid while operating outside the physical body, or in a Light Body state. I have had many out of body experiences over the years, and it is now becoming much easier for me to do this. I am also returning from my sleep state when my physical body is resting with more and more conscious memory of what I have been doing at Home in the higher dimensions while I have been there.

My home on the other side sits within an idyllic landscape on the top of a cliff overlooking the ocean, and it has the most magical views. The beauty of this place is indescribable! There is a well-worn path down to the beach, and many of my beloved animal companions greet me when I visit. It is becoming increasingly harder for me each time I go there to return here to this reality, but I know that I must. I know that I still have much more to do here, and I am not ready to say good-bye to my Loved Ones here just yet! I also know with certainty that when I am ready to leave here to return Home, there is absolutely nothing to be afraid of!

Note: To protect the privacy of my family, I do not use their names in any of my journal extracts.

Journal: April 26th 2000

My elder Granddaughter is staying with us for a few days. I have not been feeling particularly well with a sinus infection and have had trouble sleeping again. I woke up at 12:45 a.m. and could not go back to sleep. The last look at the clock said 3:20 a.m., so I relaxed down again. I started feeling sleepy, and immediately felt myself leaving my body.

I was lying slightly out of body when I became aware of cackling like laughter, which I immediately recognized as my Granddaughter's. I thought that I had better go and check on her because she should have been asleep. If the noise I was hearing was anything to go by, there appeared to be someone in her room with her. I got up out of bed, but by the time I reached the end of the bed, I realized that I was still out of body. I was floating just off the floor, so I continued to float, and then I passed straight through the closed door and into her room.

I was met by the most incredible sight. Her physical

body was still fast asleep in her bed, but her spirit, or Light Body was floating above the bed, and she was playing with other spirit children. They were playing with a ball, and my Granddaughter was laughing her little head off! There was a beautiful spirit woman, and also a young man watching over them. I am sure that it was the same woman I have seen before; she visited me before my second Granddaughter was born.

Journal: August 16th 1999

I was relaxing down ready for sleep last night when a beautiful spirit lady with long, dark blonde hair appeared to me. She smiled the most beautiful smile, and then she pressed some pink nappy pins into my right hand. I actually closed my physical hand around them as I thanked her, and then she disappeared right through me. I couldn't stop smiling! Of course when I actually looked at my hand, there was nothing there, but I could still feel the impression of them where they had pressed into my skin. I am pretty sure that there were two sets of pink pins!

August 18th

It was confirmed by ultrasound that my elder Daughter is expecting another little girl in January. I will soon have two Granddaughters to love!

CHAPTER TEN

Out of Body Experiences or O. B. E 's

Both Antoine and Lightcrow have brought to my attention the fact that at this point during our writing, you might be interested in reading about my personal Out of Body Experiences, or O. B. E`s as they are called. I have been hesitant to do this because it is not easy for me to talk about myself; however, as I was not so subtly reminded, the vibration of teaching is best felt by example, and many more of you will now be experiencing this sort of thing. It is important for you to understand that it is not "weird" in any way, but is in fact, a natural Human experience.

So here goes!

The most important thing I would like to say about this subject is that everybody leaves their physical body, whether they have conscious memory of it or not. We automatically leave it every night when we sleep...every single one of us! Our physical body rests to recharge the batteries, and our Soul, or Light Body returns to the higher dimensions to re-energize. While there, we can check in at our home, or visit our departed Loved Ones and pets, and also help in a variety of ways if that is our choice. I spontaneously started having some conscious memory of this about fifteen years ago, and this has recently accelerated. Before I go to sleep, I simply set my intention to remember, and most of the time I bring back some memory of what I have been doing there.

Most people do have some memory though because they remember their dreams, especially lucid dreams where everything seems very real. That's because it is real! During our dream state of consciousness, we interact with our departed Loved Ones, and also those people still living on the physical plane with us. We meet up in our Light Bodies. Lucid dreaming is when you are aware that you are you, and you know that you are consciously and actively participating in your dream. It is no different to being awake here on the physical plane of existence. You can easily activate all of your senses and feel all of your emotions. You may sometimes come back with a sense of both lifting and flying, or of falling. This is simply the sensation of your Light Body moving, and leaving and returning to your physical body.

You cannot get lost "out there." It is simply not possible! While your physical body is still capable of supporting life, you will always return to it because you are connected to it while you still exist in the physical world. It is your body. I have heard some people say that they have seen gossamer like silver cord, or gold filaments of Light connecting them with their physical body while they are gone. I do not disbelieve them, but this has not been my experience. I will always endeavor to only write about my own first hand experiences.

This is my Truth…this is my reality.

Time and space in the other dimensions are not like they are here. There is no time as we understand it. Time does not move there and space is not like we understand it either. We can create anything we want simply with our thought process, and we can also travel anywhere we want to with the speed of thought. We only have to think it, and we are there, but if we want to take a leisurely ride on a bike or a boat, or simply fly around in our Light Body, we can do that too!

We can also interact with all manner of animal life, including wildlife. Because there is no food chain, there is no fear attached for them. Even those species we thought extinct still exist! Please be assured when I tell you that nothing that has ever existed has ever been lost. All the pets I have ever had with me are still alive and well. I even have a beautiful Bengal Tiger and a Black Panther waiting for me there! The flowers and the trees emit music and sing, and the weather is perfect; the water is magical and the colors indescribable. Absolutely everything is infused with the soft, golden light of Unconditional Love, and Peace and Harmony abound.

How magical is that?

My husband is far more skilled with this memory thing than I am. He has full memory of everything he does there; he has had this ability since he was a young boy. His favorite place is a little island where he just loves to sit, or do some fishing, which happens to be his favorite activity in the physical world as well. He often takes me with him to his island, and we just sit together in the peace and tranquility and simply talk. As I have already mentioned, we also share a home on the other side, and many of our pets greet us upon arrival. It is possible to create any home you like...anywhere you like! My husband and I have been together for eons, but unfortunately, we don't spend as much time, or what we think of as time at our home as we would like to because of the work we have chosen to do there and here.

It may not surprise you to learn that one aspect of my chosen work while on the higher spiritual planes is to help welcome our beautiful animal companions back

Home and into the Light…especially those needing much healing and Love. A part of my husband's chosen work is Spirit Rescue…one might refer to him as a Spirit Paramedic. He helps to guide Human Souls back into the Light if they choose to…those who have lost their way, or haven't been ready to accept that they are no longer in physical form. This can sometimes happen with a traumatic "death," or when there is unfinished business the Soul considers important enough to stick around for. There is no need to be concerned about this aspect…all Souls will return to the Light when they are ready! There are many helping them, and I can assure you that they are never alone. If they have something to do that connects them to the physical plane for a bit longer, they may of course choose not to be aware of their helpers until they are ready. Remember also that time as we know it does not exist where they are, and free will always prevails. Most are just happy to return Home virtually straight away.

Travel out of body is not just limited to returning Home for visits. You can go anywhere you want to on the Earth plane as well, or go anywhere in our universe for that matter. The same thing applies; when you are out of body, you simply hold the thought of where you want to go, or who you want to see. I must point out that it doesn't have to be when you are sleeping that you are able to do this. I was merely pointing out the fact that everyone does it then. It is possible to leave your physical body even when fully awake. Some people do it while engaged in other activities as well, but I see this more as Astral Projection, and that has not been within my experience as yet.

Within my limited understanding, I believe an O. B. E is more of a spontaneous process, whereas Astral Projection is more of a deliberate or conscious action. Both have the same outcome though. Because of that, I am sure similar experiences ensue both ways. Out of body is out of body! No matter which way it is achieved, your consciousness is still operating outside your physical body.

My experience with O.B.E`s while not actually sleeping has been when I have been relaxed and in a slightly altered state of consciousness. I don't consciously leave my body; it is just something I have been doing spontaneously for many years now. But some people can do it consciously, and my husband is one of them. He just closes his eyes and relaxes down, and then he consciously leaves…day or night!

For me, this first started happening when I was guided to keep a Dream Journal about sixteen years ago.

The first few entries in my journal document my dreams, but then my dreams changed, and I started to have these experiences where I would be aware of leaving my body and going places, as well as interacting with different spirit entities. This type of experience still happens this way, and most typically will be just before sleep, or when I am waking up and still feeling relaxed and sleepy. I believe this is referred to as the hypnagogic state. It also happens when I am having a rest of an afternoon and simply relaxing down. I am not asleep, but not fully awake either. I would describe this as more of an altered state of consciousness.

Often, I don't go anywhere, and I just remain slightly out of body. I am aware that I am lying on the bed, but I am also aware of my room around me, and I can sense spirit energy. As this is happening, I often feel a weight on the bed, and I know that someone or something is with me. When I move totally out of body, I can see, hear and feel them. Conversation takes place as thought transfer. This does not frighten me at all...I love these visitations... especially when it is one or more of my beloved animals. Since I have been consciously channeling, it is happening on an almost daily basis. I guess I must have opened my window and it is now aligned with their open window. It is almost as though a portal to the other side has opened, and everyone has decided to use it and drop in for a visit to say hello!

I was recently asked how it was possible for me to feel a weight on the bed when the "visitor" would not have the weight of a physical body. I can only say that when I am interacting with other people who are also out of body, it is no different to how I interact with anyone else while we are both in the physical body. I can still feel them and hug them. I guess because I am usually out of body when this occurs, and I am operating in my Light Body the same as they are, I can feel their energy in the same way as mine. Having said that, I must also say that I have experienced this while I have been wide awake in a conscious state, and I know of many others who have experienced this also. I guess it's something I really don't know the answer to!

You should feel the bed moving when I have my boisterous pets visit!

May I give a word of caution here? In the early days of these experiences, I had a couple of what one might describe as negative encounters. Let's just say that I encountered one or two darker energy forms that were residing on the lower astral planes of existence. They were more annoyance than anything, but not something you would deliberately welcome. I believe that my reason for encountering these energies was so I would have a clear understanding that dark energy, or lowly evolved energy or thought form does indeed exist. I don't encounter them anymore, unless there is a specific reason for doing so with my work. I soon learned to ask my Guides and Angels to keep them well away from me during my travels and at all other times. Because we have free will, it is of the utmost importance that we actually ask our Guides and helpers to do this. Even Angels cannot intervene in our choice of experience without our permission, unless we are in some type of mortal danger.

I have already shared some of my personal experiences of O. B. E`s with you in preceding chapters, but I would like to include more of them here. This will take the form of my journal entries. I will endeavor to leave them exactly as they were written at the time, and add notes where it is necessary to give you a clearer understanding of them. I have written them in time sequence, which will allow you to see how they have evolved over time. This first entry is the first O.B.E I ever documented in my journal.

Journal: May 6th 1996

This was not a dream; it must have been an O.B.E because I was really there. I found myself sitting near a large window in a spacious room. It was obviously some sort of learning facility because there were a lot of old-style, wooden desks spread around. It was a lovely day with the sun shining, and I could see lots of beautiful trees around the skyline. The building appeared to be fairly old, but for some reason the windows were big, and they appeared to be fairly modern; I seemed to be on the second floor. The building was made of stone and overlooked a large square, which was also paved with stone. There was a large sculpture of a man towards one side. I remember telling myself that I had to remember that it wasn't a dream, and I was actually experiencing it. The strange thing about this is that I seemed to be aware of my physical body lying there at the same time. I knew that I was in my body and in my bed, but my consciousness was in this other place.

I would know that square and that building again anywhere!

Note: I don't know whether I had tapped into a past life, or I was experiencing an aspect of Home, or a different aspect of myself with this one.

I really don't know!

Journal: August 21st 1996

When I relaxed down this morning, I suddenly found myself outside my physical body, and I felt totally exhilarated. I met a man, who introduced himself to me as Allan. He said that he was from Daylesford in Victoria, and I asked him if he had "died." He said that he hadn't, but he had been at some party and had become bored, so he had just decided to go travelling!

Note: It was after this experience that I truly understood that one did not have to be "dead" to operate outside the physical body.

Journal: October 30th 1997

I was having an afternoon rest when I started to leave my body, and I soon became aware of voices and movement around me. I pulled myself back because I was afraid of being disturbed, but eventually decided to keep going anyway. I remained in a state where I was still aware of my surroundings, but I don't think that I was quite out of body because I felt the brush of an arm against mine. I reached out and couldn't feel anything, but then I heard flashes of conversation. I heard a male voice call out and ask me if I was asleep. I said that I wasn't, and I felt myself laughing and smiling. I felt such Love and happiness, and then I felt myself lifting, and I knew that I was leaving my body further. All of a sudden, right in front of me, a ball of bright white light appeared. As I watched, it transformed into the most beautiful white dove I have ever seen.

It had a large fantail, and it flew straight towards me and almost touched me. A beautiful water fountain appeared to my left, and the water in it was sparkling with golden white light. The dove turned and circled the fountain, and then flew straight through me! I returned to my body with a thud because one of my cats had jumped on me, but I felt happy and at peace, and I could not stop smiling!

Note: I now realize of course that the voice belonged to Antoine.

Journal: December 16th 1997

I was lying in bed this morning half asleep when I felt a kiss on my cheek. I got a bit of a fright and jumped! I thought my husband must have done it, but when I opened my eyes and turned and looked at him, he was fast asleep with his back to me.

Note: I have had this happen again on other occasions. I receive these special little kisses on a fairly regular basis!

I have also felt a kick in the backside, which made me jump! I don't know what that was all about!

I was settling down for sleep one night when I actually saw, and then felt a hand grab hold of my left wrist and pull back on it, as though it was trying to stop me from doing something, or warning me to slow down. I got such a fright that I jumped then too!

I have also been woken up at times with things being moved around on my bedside table.

My music box often starts playing for me while I am trying to have a rest in my bedroom, but the thing is…it has not been wound up for years!

I love it when these things happen!

I know that they are just letting me know that they are

around me.

Journal: January 24th 1998

I left my body about 4:30 a.m. this morning. I remember realizing that I was out of body and I decided to experiment. I rose to the ceiling, and then I floated out into the living room where I saw my husband lying on the couch. He had gone out there about half an hour earlier because he was awake and disturbing me. I passed through the closed back door, and then I rose right up into the night sky; from there I looked down onto the house and trees. I decided I was going to go and see Mum and Dad, but all of a sudden I couldn't see anymore, so I decided to come back into my body.

Journal: February 26th 1998

I became aware during the night that I had been taken away somewhere. I was lying down in some sort of healing environment, and I am pretty sure that it must have been on the other side because it was nothing like we have here. There were two Beings of Light with me, and I remember saying to one of them that I'd had enough of feeling sick. She told me that the worst was yet to come. I asked her when that would be; she said that April would be my worst month. I was upset because April is my birthday and it is my favorite month. She said that she was sorry, but unfortunately that was just the way it had to be. I looked up and saw the other Being bring some sort of instrument down towards my face. I remember feeling a bit frightened because I thought that it was going to pierce my eye, but I don't remember anything after that.

Note: In late March 1998, I was diagnosed with thyroid cancer and my first operation was scheduled for 19th April. I spent my birthday on 16th April at the hospital, attending my pre-operation appointment.

Journal: March 9th 1998

I drifted into an altered state early this morning, and I was shown a beautiful blue quilt. It was dark blue with a pattern of yellow or gold stars and a moon on it. It reminded me of a universe, but it was unusual because it appeared to be done in large squares like a quilt.

Journal: March 26th 1998.

I had my gastroscopy today ready for surgery. When I was emerging from the sedation and the nurse was trying to wake me, I looked past her and saw this same quilt. When I was totally awake, I asked her about it, but she had absolutely no idea what I was talking about. I had thought that it was really there, but it was nowhere to be seen.

Journal: October 12th 1998

While I was out of body early this morning, I met a man called Joe. He was a very melancholy Soul. I guess that he just isn't ready to move on yet. He seemed sad, but he didn't say what had happened to him. He just told me that he had been killed in 1937. He was in his thirties and had reddish, blonde hair, a fair complexion with blue eyes, and a moustache.

Note: If I met Joe today, I would know how to help him into the Light if that was his choice. Unfortunately, back then, I did not have a clue!

Journal: October 26th 1998

I couldn't sleep after receiving an upsetting phone call. I felt myself leaving my body, and for the first time, I realized that I could control my actions. I learned how to open my spirit eyes properly, and I could see more clearly than before.

I was drawn back towards my body, and I was shown a black tunnel, which I sped through. I was able to look out into the Light at the other end. It was like tunnel vision, or looking through a single binocular, and I saw great mounds, or hills of what appeared to be white colored rock. All over these hills, there were young men working with some kind of a tool, which looked similar to a pick. When they hit the mounds with the tools, it was obvious to me that they were made of something much softer than rock. The men all had dark, longish hair and muscular bronzed bodies, and they wore short, beige colored skirts with brown colored sandals; they did not wear any shirts. I watched the scene for some time and felt really elated! For some reason, the scene felt very familiar to me. I have a vague memory of someone actually in the tunnel with me while I was travelling through it. He was dressed differently to them though, and when he saw me, he took off in fright!

Note: I was telling my husband about this the next day. He suggested to me that the early Egyptians may have worked in this way cutting blocks of salt. That would make sense, but why was I seeing it? Was this a glimpse into a previous life perhaps?

Journal: November 12th 1998

I could not get back to sleep very early this morning, so I rolled onto my side and my husband cuddled into my back with his arm around my waist. Eventually, I felt myself leaving my body. Suddenly, I realized that I was flying, and it felt fantastic! I saw that my husband was with me, and he was still holding me around the waist. I looked around and below me, and I felt absolutely euphoric!

There was a landscape the like of which I have never experienced before, and the light was different also; it was like a clear golden color. The colors of everything were very vivid...incredible greens and gold's. There were russet and gold colored pine trees everywhere, and the sky was an unusual blue color; although the colors were really vivid, it was like looking through a filtered photographic lens. When I looked down, I saw a lake or a sea there, and the water was like nothing I have ever seen before - smooth like glass, and perfectly clear. There were some beautiful old wooden ships with a lot of small, white sails unfurled on them, floating on the water; they reminded me of pirate ships!

As we continued flying, we saw an old building below us; it reminded me of old ruins, and appeared to be made from some kind of smooth rock. We flew into a window-like opening, and then realized that we needn't have because there was no roof! Inside, there was what appeared to be a number of monks, who were dressed in some sort of ceremonial robes. We were laughing because we thought that they couldn't see us, but it soon became evident that they could, so we departed! They seemed to be really surprised to see us, and we did not want to disturb them further. We flew around a bit more, and then I suddenly realized that I was back in my body. I was still in the same position as when I left with my husband's arm around my waist.

I turned around to look at him. He opened his eyes and smiled at me, and then he asked me if I had enjoyed our "trip" together!

Note: He has taken me with him on other "trips" to the higher dimensions since then, but this one remains the most memorable for me because it is the first conscious memory I ever retained of the exquisite colors and landscape to be experienced there.

Journal: October 9th 1999

I was dozing early this morning when I felt myself "going." Suddenly, I heard a lot of chatter, and then I realized that I was hearing children's voices. They were very excited that I had made contact with them, and they were actually yelling so loudly in my ear that it hurt! One female voice became very clear to me, and I asked her who she was. She said that her name was Annette and she was nineteen years old. As my spirit vision became clearer, I saw a young girl hovering to the left of me. She appeared to be very shy. When I spoke to her, she didn't answer me, so I don't know who she was, but she was about five years old, and she had short, sandy blonde hair and slightly protruding front teeth. She finally came up to me and shyly hugged me, and then proceeded to sit on my lap for some time. She then passed straight through me! When I came back from the altered state, I felt absolutely exuberant, and I have remained that way all day.

Note: These experiences involving children are really special. I know with certainty that they are never lost to us, and that they love to make contact with us. Thankfully, they are also cared for by loving Souls, such as Annette.

Journal: January 5ᵗʰ 2001

My husband had gone into the spare room to get some sleep because I was having a bad night, and I was disturbing him. I felt ill with a sore throat. Suddenly, I found myself out of body, and I was amazed to see his spirit body still asleep beside me. I rolled over and gave him a hug and a kiss, which he returned in kind. I asked him if he wanted to go flying with me, but he declined. I couldn't decide whether to go through the ceiling, or the bedroom wall, but then I decided that it didn't really matter, so I went with the ceiling. I remember seeing the rafters in the roof, and then I found myself outside in the night sky, surrounded by stars. I felt absolutely ecstatic, and I just floated there for ages, in a state of pure bliss.

Note: As you can probably gather from this account, I was beginning to be more comfortable with all of this, and I was also beginning to have a little bit of fun with it!

Journal: March 11th 2001

I was woken up at 1:30 a.m. and couldn't go back to sleep, so at 3: 00 a.m. I decided to get up for a while. Eventually, I went back to bed again and immediately felt myself "going;" I was actually conscious of leaving my body. I felt myself rise up, and then felt the sensation of travelling very quickly. I heard a noise, but for some reason I pulled back. I asked my Guides to help me to keep going. Immediately, I heard a child's cackling laugh, and I recognized it as belonging to my elder Granddaughter; then I heard the little noise my younger Granddaughter makes and I knew that she was there too. All of a sudden, I felt another presence, and I realized that my older Daughter was there as well! I felt such Love for the three of them, and I felt very peaceful and happy. I could feel myself still smiling as I came back into my physical body.

Note: It is magical when you realize that you can visit

with your family and Loved Ones like this. It doesn't matter how far away from you they live because distance is no barrier when you visit in this way.

This demonstrates that it really doesn't matter whether your Loved Ones have already gone Home to the other side, or whether they are still here with you on the physical plane, they are still accessible to you, and you actually visit each other often, whether you realize it or not!

Journal: April 14th 2001

I felt myself leaving my body again during the night, and then found myself with my younger Daughter. She looked so radiant and beautiful; she wore a pale blue halter neck sundress with a design of some sort on it, and she was just as she is at the moment with her long dark hair. She held her arms out towards me, and we hugged and kissed; I felt so happy to see her. I know we spoke for some time, but unfortunately, I have no memory of what the conversation was about!

Note: This is another example of visiting with a Loved One who is still "alive" on the Earth plane.

Journal: December 22nd 2002

About 4:30 a.m. I felt a distinct kiss on my left cheek... twice! At first, I thought that it was my husband getting me up for our early morning walk because he always kisses me on the cheek to do that. In my half asleep state, I looked at the alarm clock, and then realized that it was too early for that; he was still asleep anyway! The kisses felt very familiar to me, and then I remembered that it was my younger Granddaughter's third birthday today.

Note: She had actually arrived into our world two weeks earlier than her expected January birth date and it didn't take much to work out who this was! It is natural for young children to consciously maintain their connection to their spirit bodies. Visiting me like this on her birthday because she lived so far away from me at the time would have been a very easy and natural thing for her to do! Love is the connection here, and it is important to remember that a child might look like a child, but behind the facade is often in fact, a very old and wise Soul. This is especially so with my Granddaughter's generation.

Journal: December 27th 2002

I found myself out of body during the night, and I could feel sadness and despair all around me. There were a lot of people there, and I think that they were mainly male. They were walking in a line, but there was a lot of space between each of them. They seemed to be walking with a purpose, but I couldn't see where they were going. I went up to one of them and tried to comfort him, but he virtually ignored me. He was probably in his forties with graying, curly hair, and he was dressed in a black dinner suit with the collar undone on his white shirt. He also had a black bow tie hanging loosely around his neck. He looked disheveled and appeared to be confused, as though he had been involved with some kind of trauma. He just kept walking aimlessly. I don't remember any more.

Note: I believe that this would be the kind of situation my husband helps with.

There were a few years following these entries when most of my experiences involved visitations with my adored Parents and my beloved Pets, but they are so special that they deserve to be shared in separate chapters further on.

Journal: March 14th 2008

I felt myself leaving my body early this morning, but for some reason I couldn't keep going, so I asked my Guides to help me. I immediately felt two hands hold onto mine and pull me; I was virtually pulled out of my body! I actually felt the sensation of being dragged along, and then they pushed my hands together and started to clap them. I felt them pull away, but I continued clapping. I felt really happy, and I could feel them smiling at me; they were congratulating me and saying "Well done!"

Note: I think that this was because by this time, I seemed to be more consciously aware of the process. I was learning to control it, and for a while there I was a little bit "spooked" by that aspect and had a tendency to hold back. I think that they were telling me that they were proud of my achievements so far.

Journal: October 9th 2009

I was lying on my side early this morning when I felt myself drifting into an altered state. I became aware of someone beside me, and as I reached out, I felt an arm resting on the pillow above my head. I knew by the muscular feel to it that it was a male. I looked up and behind me, and I saw a very handsome man looking lovingly down at me. He had the darkest brown eyes with a dark complexion and very dark hair. I felt that I knew him, and I asked him who he was, but he didn't answer me. He just said that he had wanted to visit me before this, but he couldn't just use the portals as he wished because they were being used for very important work now. I know that he stayed for some time and we spoke, but I obviously drifted into sleep, and when I woke up, I had no memory of the actual conversation, and he was gone.

Note: When these visitors appear in my bedroom, I am no longer surprised...I now expect them. These visits have escalated to the point where most mornings, as soon as my husband leaves the bedroom and all is quiet and peaceful, I just allow myself to drift, and the portal opens.

Perhaps I am opening it myself!

I will finish this chapter with two of the most recent and most beautiful visitations it has been my privilege to experience. The second one is different in as much as it is double edged. It is a vision, and then a visitation as well. This one is indicative of how these experiences have accelerated and evolved since I have been working with my Guides on a conscious level. The meaning is self-explanatory.

Journal June 8th 2010

I was drifting off again this morning with my two little dogs on the bed with me when I actually felt myself lifting higher and leaving my body. I became aware of a swirling pattern like a vortex above me, and I lifted into it. The next thing I knew, I was sitting at the old dining room table that we had owned when I was a child. My parents and my younger brother were there also, but my older sister was not. My brother was about fourteen, so that would make sense because when he was that age, my sister would have already left home. We were eating a salad, and I remember thinking how strange it was to be eating a salad when I was waiting for my husband to bring my toast and coffee into me in the bedroom. This he does every morning. I even noticed Mum's plate was empty because she had finished hers. She said she would pick up some meat for tea on her way home from work. She often did that.

I was very obviously re-visiting a scene from my past.

That is all I can remember, except for the fact that I was feeling around the bed for my two little dogs. I felt them with their little coats on, but there was also another dog without a coat on there with them. This was obviously one of my previous dogs come to visit, but I have absolutely no idea which one!

Journal: July 24th 2010

I drifted into an altered state early this morning, and I found myself experiencing a vision in which a young woman told me that she was "The Keeper of the Lake." She told me her name, but I can't remember what it was! She had short, dark blonde hair and wore a floral dress. She explained to me that she had chosen to drown in this lake, in order to become its keeper, and then, right in front of me, she walked into the lake and slowly sank from view.

As I looked away, I became aware of something very large looming towards me through the portal into my bedroom. It soon became evident to me that it was a very large tiger. At first I thought that it was my Bengal Tiger, but this one was different. I became anxious because I didn't know this one, and even in an altered state, I am very much aware that I can still feel pain. I was a bit worried that he might make a meal of me! I needn't have worried though because he came up beside me and lay down with his head next to mine. He was of a massive size! He looked into my eyes and transferred the knowledge to me that there were only 1,256 of his species left on this planet. He then closed his eyes and slept pressed up against me for a while. I was also aware of another one that I presumed was the female, sitting further back, patiently waiting for him.

After a while he left, and I became aware of caged birds all around me. They were the kind you would see in bird shows. There was a yellow canary and a green budgerigar, and I remember someone asking me if I could please look after them. I don't remember anymore because my husband interrupted by bringing in my breakfast; however, this incredible experience does not end there!

Because I was given such specific information by this magnificent animal about the plight of his species, I decided that I would do a bit of research on the Internet. I looked up tigers in general, and found that most of them were running low in numbers. Eventually, I thought that it must have been a Bengal after all.

I decided that I would give it a miss and not worry about it, so I tried to leave the page I was looking at. Tried is the word! Every time I tried to leave, the page would flick back! This happened three times before I heard Antoine say: *Take more notice Child!*

My eye caught a link I had previously missed in the left hand corner. It was for information on The Siberian Tiger, and it was my tiger!

Mystery solved!

This magnificent creature's demise is very imminent unless something can be done to help them. I believe that he may have been a "spokesman" for the whole tiger population.

Perhaps someone out there is wise enough to know how to do this?

I pray so!

CHAPTER ELEVEN

Cyclone Yasi

February 2nd 2011

There has been a severe cyclone watch in North Queensland for days now, and at about 2 a.m. we understood that a very serious situation had developed there. When I woke up this morning, I turned on the television and immediately saw the weather system on the map. As I did, I recognized the familiar feeling in the pit of my stomach that I always feel as a warning to me that something is not quite right.

As I stood in the kitchen feeding the animals, I started to receive the following channel from Antoine. As usual, this was given to me for my understanding, but this time it involved some of my valued friends, so I immediately passed it on to them as well.

Antoine

Child, we have already explained to you how Mother Earth is undertaking a massive clearing out of Her old energies.

The ancient land you have chosen to inhabit during this lifetime holds much negative energy. This extends way back beyond your understanding of time, but even within your Human understanding of time there is much to be cleared. We have told you before that there is much more to come with these weather patterns, and the clearing out of these old energies.

You must understand that there is more within the elemental structure than water and fire. You also have the elements of air and earth within your makeup, but we are telling you now that there is a fifth element, and that element is Ether. It is the master element that is everything that is, and it can be changed…transformed at will! Mother Earth will use whatever She has available to Her to help facilitate this clearing process.

You look at these images now on your television screen, and you feel agitation and disquiet within your being. Listen to your feelings Child! There is much more to come. It is not for you to know where, or when this will happen, but we can tell you that there is more for your ancient land to experience. There is more loss to bear, and more Human sorrow. We ask you to send your Love force out from your heart center and into those areas where it is needed most at this time. This is necessary Child! You know that you are Support, and you will be there to support as always.

If you feel the need in your heart to tell your friends these words; then do so. This is not a validation that they will be affected; this is simply a validation that what you are feeling is correct.

We ask you to connect with Mother Earth and send much Love to Her because She is in crisis, and this is not just where you are. There are in fact many crisis points ready to erupt all over your planet. This will happen in different ways and at different times, but it is all happening quickly now within your Human understanding of how time moves.

Out of all this much good comes, but during the process there will also be much sorrow, sadness and agitation. Be still Child; be calm and send your Love out into the world; this is your task...your destiny. We Love you and support you, and we know that you Love and support your friends in a deep and profound way. They know within them what they must do, and they will act on those feelings. They have much guidance of their own, and they will listen to it.

We honor you Child, and we are here to help you in

any way we can.

Be still.

Be peaceful.

Be the calm within the storm.

We Love you so much!

February 3rd 2011

I went to bed last night still experiencing a sense of disquiet within my whole being. I felt very uneasy about tropical cyclone Yasi bearing down on Queensland. It is a category 5, and it is massive! It was due to cross the coast about midnight, and I knew that I was feeling the outpouring of emotion and fear from this area. Earlier in the day, I had received a vision depicting a scene of destruction, which also involved people being hurt, and this had affected me also.

I must have eventually fallen into a fitful sleep because I have vague memories of doing something, but I can't remember exactly what.

I woke-up about 1:30 a.m. (Tasmanian daylight saving time), and as I headed to the bathroom, I realized that although I still felt incredibly tired, I actually felt calm and peaceful. I sensed a shift of energy within me and around me, and I was able to manage a few more hours sleep.

When I woke-up this morning, I was absolutely amazed by the images greeting me on the television screen. It was nothing like I had expected! At this point in my writing there has been no loss of life...not even a serious injury, even though it was the largest and most ferocious cyclone that Queensland has experienced in living history with destructive winds of up to 320 kilometers per hour at its center. There was simply no logical explanation for this seemingly miraculous outcome.

I immediately heard Antoine`s words in my ear.

Antoine

You appear surprised and a little confused Child? Have you not yet grasped the concept of who you truly are?

You are Human yes, with Human capabilities, but are you not also a body of Light? You are also in effect particles of the master element, and you can enter into energy and transform it with your own energy at will. You have the ability to affect and change that which is also Ether...the Essence...everything that is. You are learning this at a fast rate! When enough of you understand this concept and come together with pure intent and the powerful Light of one force...then it is possible to enter into and manipulate the energy of anything you choose.

Is this not what you might term magic?

We are telling you Child: You are all magicians!

We also offer you a glimpse of another concept you are yet to understand, and that is that you also have the ability to "bend" time as you know it. This has the potential for you to change the outcome of an event at will. When you have mastered this concept, you will have finally become the architect of your own world and your own destiny. This will be the way of your future; this is who you truly are!

I will move aside now Child, and allow Lightcrow to expand upon this awareness.

Lightcrow: February 3rd 2011

Greetings Dear Ones,

We have spoken with you and given you some understanding of how everything, including your Light

Body is comprised of energy, and that this energy is all connected; it is all One, and it can be altered and transformed at will.

You are now being taken to a new level of understanding within this concept. You are now being shown in a profound and experiential way that you are capable of using your own energetic power to perform that which you would term miracles. You are indeed incredible creators, and many of you are finally waking up and gaining an understanding of this. You are remembering who you truly are, and why you are there at this time. You are helping with the process of creating your Heaven on Earth!

We are witnessing a wondrous event from our vantage point. We are watching those whom you would term the Lightworkers of your planet, consciously joining their energetic fields and working as one with the spiritual energies, to bring balance into the clearing process that Mother Earth is undertaking. There are now enough of you awake to make this possible. The tide is indeed turning!

More and more of you are starting to realize that you are so much more than that flotsam and jetsam floating around on the planet at the mercy of Mother Nature. You have now reached a level of awareness that allows you to understand that because your energy is of the very same essence as your atmosphere itself, you are capable of entering into and altering that energy, no matter what the conditions might be. You are working in harmony with the Nature Spirits and Mother Earth Herself, in a glorious act of co-creation to bring this about. You are starting to realize that you can change the intensity, and therefore the outcome of these weather events. You are learning that you can create and mould your own outcomes. You are now beginning to create your New World in a conscious collaboration with Mother Earth Herself.

You cannot and would not prevent this clearing process from occurring because it is important and necessary work, and you all understand that at some level, but you can alter the events in such a way that minimal impact will be felt by all who inhabit your planet. The weather event you have just experienced, or witnessed would have been much more destructive if there had not been this intervention, and there are those capable of thinking only with the logical mind, who will not be able to understand why this was not so.

It is important to remember that the process of Human connection must be allowed to take place at this time also.

Human Beings connect well through the common thread of adversity, and the clearing out of the old energies will facilitate that connection process in a new and profound way.

We say to you now that the potential was there for great loss of Human life. You did not allow that to happen, but instead you helped manipulate the energies to bring about the best possible outcome for Humanity and your planet.

Can you imagine the incredible power this took to achieve? You are learning that your power is equal to that of the Nature Spirits; you are indeed no less! You are learning to work with the natural energies and not against them as in the past, so that a place of balance and harmony can be reached with Mother Earth with minimal destruction and sorrow for Humanity.

This same concept can be used for the many different situations developing throughout your world at this time. If enough of you work together with your Light and the power that you hold within, you have the ability to transform and to help clear the negative energies from these potentially volatile situations.

We know that you can achieve this.

We have great faith in you all!

We watch in awe as we witness the incredible role you have chosen to play in this co-creation process, and we say to you all: Well done!

Note: This is not the first time I have witnessed an energy shift within a potentially disastrous situation, but until now, I did not understand what had actually taken place at that time.

In March 2005 I had a vivid dream, which unfortunately became a reality in December of 2006, not long after we made our move from Queensland to the beautiful East Coast of Tasmania. At the time of this dream, we had not even taken the holiday to Tasmania that had precipitated our decision to move there permanently.

Journal: March 4ᵗʰ 2005

I had another vivid dream early this morning. I was with my husband, and we were standing outside another house; this house was very old and appeared to be up high. All of a sudden, I noticed ash and burning leaves falling from the sky. I said to my husband that there must be a fire, and it must be very close. He told me that there couldn't be because he had not been notified; he has been a volunteer Fire-Fighter for years. It got worse, so we went inside and looked out a side window. There was a lot of bush around, but we could see directly out across a beautiful blue bay with a white beach, and on the other side of the bay we could see a bright orange glow. We could distinctly see a massive bushfire burning right down to the beach. My husband said that he didn't want a fire coming from that direction, and that we might have to get out.

Note: There is no doubt in my mind that this dream was a prophetic one.

After we had finally made our decision to move, we bought a beautiful, old, late Victorian home in the centre of a very pretty village with a unique location. Our town sits within a valley on top of a mountain range, just behind the ocean, and we are a short ten minute drive down the mountain to the beautiful East Coast beaches. What happened on December 6th 2006 is still hard to fathom. What started as a careless act of lighting a campfire on an extremely hot day, and then not making sure that it was extinguished properly turned into an inferno of huge proportions.

As a volunteer Fire-Fighter my husband was out on the front line, and during those first hours I didn't know whether I would ever see him again. The fire was racing through the forest surrounding our home, and it was being fuelled by high, hot winds. For two days our town was in jeopardy, and we had ash and burning leaves falling all around our house; for two days I had our pets in close proximity to their carry cages, and the car packed.

We were eventually told that we were in the direct path of the fire, and it was bearing down on us. We had to make the decision to leave our home, or to stay, but just as plans were put into place for our evacuation, there was a shift in energy, and an unexplained change in the direction of the wind.

My husband and I both felt this energy shift, but he felt it on a more profound level than me because he was out there, interacting with the fire itself in a direct way, at the time this was happening. He has always told me that fire is a living entity, and that it thinks. I have every reason to believe that he is right.

Our town was spared, but the beautiful seaside village near us on the coast was not. It tore through there like a freight train, and burned right down to the beach; the sand was even on fire! Many properties were lost there, as well as others that were taken further up the coast in the first hours of this raging inferno. Sadly, there was one fatality…a young forestry worker, who was hit by a falling tree during the clean-up process.

If the direction of this bushfire had not been altered, our whole town would have been lost, along with a large percentage of our residents.

There is absolutely no doubt in my mind about that.

CHAPTER TWELVE

Transition

B oth Antoine and Lightcrow have indicated to me that the most important message or Higher Truth they wish to present to you at this particular time is an understanding that no matter how your Loved Ones make their transition to the other side, whether you might judge it to be peaceful or traumatic, they are never lost to you. This understanding is especially relevant and necessary for Humanity at this time of great change upon our planet when so many of us have chosen to go Home, rather than to remain here during this shift in consciousness.

To this end, they have asked me to share some of my own visitations with my departed Loved Ones. I am sure that there are many of you who have had similar experiences. I believe it is of great importance to them once they leave this plane of existence that they let us know in some way that they do still consciously exist, and that they are in fact, very much alive and well!

I would also like to share with you how both my parents made their transitions to the other side.

My Father

My parents were both good and loving people. They made their transitions to the other side four years apart; they were both around the age of seventy-eight. If one believes in coincidence, they were also born four years apart. I do not believe in coincidence. I believe that everything happens for a reason. It is also my belief that we enter into agreements or contracts with other Souls before we incarnate here on the Earth plane. We also incarnate in Soul groups time and time again, in order to help each other along our spiritual path. The link between us is Love, and this was especially evident between my parents. Their Soul connection was so strong that they simply could not bear to be apart for too long. My Father was the first to make his transition; it has now been more than a decade, and I still miss him terribly.

He suffered greatly in his last few years from the effects of heart disease, and after undergoing heart surgery for five bypasses, which was later followed by a lower leg amputation, he grew weary. Finally, he suffered another heart attack, and he was hospitalized once again. He appeared to be recovering, but one night at midnight, just after he had been in hospital for a week or so, I received a phone call from my mother. She told me that Dad had asked the nurses to call her. He had told them that he knew that he was dying, and he wanted Mum with him. My husband and I also headed for the hospital.

When we arrived, we found him to be in good spirits, and he seemed to be quite alert despite having been administered morphine. I asked him if he had decided to leave us all, and I told him that it was O.K. if he had. He gave me a big grin, and told me that he had changed his mind and had decided to stay, but I sensed that he was just trying to make us feel better because my husband told me that he could see a beautiful blonde spirit woman with him. She was holding his hand, and she told him that she was there to take Dad home. She was aware that my husband could see her, but she just continued to smile lovingly at us all.

We sat with him throughout the night, talking with him and watching over him while he dozed. About 4 a.m. while he was sleeping, Mum asked my husband if he would take her to their home, which was only a few minutes away, so she could have a shower and change her clothes. When they arrived at the house, she couldn't find her house keys. She had used them to lock the screen door the previous night, and had then put them in her handbag before heading to the hospital. She searched the car in case they had fallen out, but they were nowhere to be found. Finally, she used the set she kept hidden outside to gain entry to the house.

While she attended to the things she wanted to do, my husband pulled out a dining chair, intending to sit down and wait for her. It was the chair my Father always used, and it had not been used by anyone since he had been in hospital. As he did so, he noticed something on the seat. In total amazement, he realized that what he was looking at were the missing house keys! There is no logical explanation for what happened. The keys had to have been used to lock the security screen door to the house. Somehow, Dad had moved those keys from Mum's handbag and put them on his chair at home while he was sleeping in his hospital bed. I believe that he made that journey to their home with her in his Light Body, and he was simply letting her know that he was there with her!

Dad was stirring when they arrived back at the hospital, and they related the incident to us. I don't think that he disbelieved them, but he seemed a bit confused, and he didn't have much to say about it either; he changed the subject by asking whether everything was alright at home.

About 6 a.m. he asked me to get everyone on the phone for him, so that he could say his goodbyes. He spoke to my brother and sister, and then to both of my daughters, thanking them for their love, and bidding them farewell. As you can imagine, it was extremely emotional for all of us, but he remained calm and focused throughout. His doctor arrived about 7 a.m. and confirmed what we already knew. Just before 8 a.m. Dad asked me for a cup of tea. He loved nothing more than a cup of strong, black tea with three teaspoons of sugar in it! I asked him if he had decided whether he was going to leave us yet, and he told me that "they" had told him that he couldn't stay this time.

He had clinically died four years earlier when he had his leg amputated, but had been resuscitated. He always told us that he couldn't remember anything about it, but I remember him asking me at the time who all the people were around him in the hospital room. He even went so far as to say that he didn't know some of them. Of course there was no-one in the room with us in a physical sense, but he had obviously communicated with some-one in spirit form, and at that time he had chosen to stay.

I held him while he sipped his tea, and after a few sips he started to cough. We sat him up, but he was already gone from us. I felt his Light Body exit his physical body, and then there was nothing. I feel extremely blessed to have been a part of this very personal and sacred process, and I feel very proud and humbled to have chosen a Soul so special to be my beloved Father during this lifetime.

I was extremely close to my Dad, and he would often call me "Sweetie Pie." Three weeks after his passing, I was trying to have an afternoon rest when I heard him say: Hello Sweetie Pie! It was so loud, and so unexpected that I nearly jumped out of my skin! He appeared to me again a few weeks later while I was slightly out of body, and this time he held my face in his hands. I covered his hands with my own, and I felt tremendous Love flowing from him to me.

My Mother

My adored Mother's transition could not have been more different, or more difficult; my heart ached for her. She had been diagnosed with renal failure, but after consultation with my sister and brother, as well as with me, she made the decision not to have dialysis. She just simply did not want that quality of life, and she missed Dad so much; she just wanted to be with him!

She tried really hard to move on, and she made new friends, but the spark had gone from her. Her health deteriorated to the point where she decided to sell her house and move in with me and my husband, so we could care for her. After working as a therapist in the aged care sector for many years, I was determined that she would not go into care. This move was supported by her Doctors, but it was a very hard thing for her to do. She had to leave behind the last home she had made with her beloved husband, and it quite literally broke her heart.

We spent the last ten months of her earthly life sharing memories, and just being together and loving each other, but it was difficult for all of us, and due to my health issues as well as those of my husband, we could no longer care for her when she finally became bedridden.

Because we lived on a property half an hour's drive from the private hospital she had always used, it was decided that the best thing to do for all concerned would be to hospitalize her. We all knew that her transition was imminent, and it would not be for very long. This was a very difficult decision to make because it was her greatest wish that she remain with us in our home. In some ways, I still struggle with the decision I had to make at that time.

I had advised the nursing staff that I wanted to be with her when she passed; sadly that never happened. I visited her daily, and witnessed her deterioration with a great sense of loss and sadness within my heart. After two weeks, she became comatose, and a few days later my Sister arrived to sit with her for the day. I did not see Mum that day; I wanted my Sister to have her special time with her on her own. After spending the night with us at our home, my Sister visited Mum again the next morning, before embarking on the return journey to her own home. My husband and I arrived at the hospital just before she left, and we remained with Mum for some time. Finally, after giving her a kiss and telling her how much we loved her, we left; we told her we would see her again the next day, but sadly that never happened.

Strangely, or not so strangely, this was to be her last day with us.

During her last days, Mum had developed a very sweet smell, not unlike the scent of violets. This was unmistakable, and the moment you walked into the hospital room, you became aware of it. My sister had a two and a half hour drive back to her home, but she rang me long before she reached it; she told me that she had to pull over because she had become too emotional to continue driving. About half an hour into her drive, the car had filled with this particular scent. Apparently Mum had decided to ride with her and make sure that she got safely home! The scent stayed in the car until she reached her destination, and then it disappeared.

I do believe that the Light Body is fully conscious and free to roam when the physical body is in a comatose state, and that is why it is so important to keep interacting with our Loved Ones if they are experiencing this state of consciousness, even though they may appear not to be aware of anything, or anyone.

I was extremely tired, so after checking with the hospital to make sure that there had been no change, I went to bed as usual, thinking that I would spend the next day just sitting with my Mum. We were woken by the phone about 1:20 a.m. It was the hospital telling us that Mum had taken a turn for the worst, and if I wanted to be with her when she passed, I had better hurry. We quickly dressed and arrived at the hospital at 1:50 a.m.

We were ten minutes too late.

As we walked into her room, we were aware of the fact that it was totally empty. Although my darling Mother was still in her bed, we sensed no energy there; she certainly hadn't stuck around for long! We stayed with her for about forty-five minutes anyway, and as I cried my tears, we said our final good-byes. Eventually, we headed back home to make the necessary phone calls to family.

During the last days of her illness, we were aware that there were many spirit people with her in that hospital room. Her parents were there constantly, and so was my Father, but there were also other family members coming and going, as well as some people I didn't recognize.

I wish things had been different; I wish I had just gone back to the hospital and sat it out with her to the end. After all, I had seen all the signs before because I had witnessed it many times with my work. I will never understand why I didn't do that. I spent a long time beating myself up over it, but I have finally come to the conclusion that I just wasn't meant to be with her...for whatever reason.

I also know that she did not make that final trip alone. She had a hospital room full of loving family with her, and her beloved husband was there to guide her safely Home!

My husband had also seen my Father a couple of weeks earlier. He had come to tell us that it was not going to be too long before he and Mum would be together again. He showed himself as a young man standing beside a bicycle, and he was holding onto a toffee apple to give to her. I do not know the significance of that! When I was growing up, we did not own a car for many years, and bicycles were our only mode of transport, so perhaps it had something to do with that. Even though Mum was not able to comprehend much, or communicate lucidly because she was on high doses of morphine, as well as other pain killing injections at that point, we did tell her about it. She smiled, so perhaps the meaning was not lost on her, and I am sure that it must have brought her some degree of comfort.

Because she had become too weak to call out, we had given Mum a small brass bell to ring when she needed us. This was especially useful at night. For the last three days we cared for her at home, she would ring it constantly - all through the night as well!

We arrived home from the hospital just after 3 a.m. After making phone calls to my sister and my daughters, we tried to get a little more rest to help us cope with the exhausting day ahead. I was starting to doze about 4 a.m. when I distinctly heard that brass bell ring! I jumped, and then thought that I must have imagined it. I turned to my husband, and as I started to tell him about it…it rang again! This time we both heard it. I had asked her to let me know somehow when she was safely Home on the other side; she did that beautifully!

I felt a small amount of comfort with this contact, and I was able to doze for a couple of hours. When I awoke about 6:30 a.m., my husband told me that his Pop, who is often with him, came for him about 5 a.m. and took him out of body to see her on the other side. She was walking hand in hand with Dad along a pathway; there were some gardens there, and they both appeared to be young again. She wore a floral dress, and he was wearing a pale blue shirt with dark trousers. He was pointing out various flowers to her, and they both looked so happy; both of them were bathed in a beautiful, soft, golden light.

When I put on my wristwatch to go out later that day, I happened to notice that it had lost almost three quarters of an hour. This was the exact amount of time I had spent with Mum in the hospital room after she had died. I adjusted the time, thinking that it probably just needed a new battery…it worked perfectly, and it has done ever since!

Three days after my Mother's departure from this physical world, I had a lucid dream with her in it. She appeared to me wearing the nightgown in which she had "died." She told me that she would not be leaving me, and she would be around me most of the time. She also told me that my husband and I would be able to see her at times, and that she very definitely was not "dead"; she was in fact, very much alive and well!

In another lucid dream a few days later, she appeared to me wearing a favorite dress of hers, which I had planned to give to her friend the very next day. I am sure that she was telling me that she knew what I was going to do with it! She was opening the refrigerator in my kitchen, exactly as she had done on many occasions during the months she had lived with us.

The next morning, after my husband had left the bedroom, I was dozing and slightly out of body when I felt a strong presence around me. At first, I thought that my husband must have returned to bed, but I realized that he couldn't have because I was on my side with my back to the edge of the bed, and this was where I was feeling the presence. I felt Mum's hand take hold of my right hand. She lovingly caressed it, and as I opened my spirit eyes, I saw her. I mentally asked her to talk to me, and I told her how much I loved her and missed her. She didn't answer me, but simply squeezed my hand instead.

My face was covered in tears, and I was still sobbing with emotion when my husband brought my breakfast in to me.

Note: My brother, who is a bit of a skeptic about these things admitted to me that he had felt a distinct presence in the bedroom with him at about 1:45 a.m., and he had also noticed that he felt intensely cold all over. He had asked me earlier that night not to ring him again if Mum had already passed when I got to the hospital, so as not to wake and upset his young family; he had no idea of what time she had gone. I did not ring him to tell him that she had passed over until 6:30 the next morning.

I have had many visitations with both my beloved parents during the years since their return Home to the other side...some separately, and some together. I will share some of these with you in the next chapter.

I have also had visitations from other spirit people, who I have had a connection with in some way while they were here on the Earth plane of existence. One of these was with a dear lady who was a great friend to our family. She had three sons, but no daughters, and she always treated me like the daughter she never had; I always referred to her as my Aunt. She was always buying me little gifts, and passing on her cooking tips to me. When she passed, I had not seen her for a number of years because I lived so far away from her. She was unable to make contact with me because she suffered from Alzheimer's disease, and she did not remember anyone.

She passed over just before my birthday in April 2002. Shortly afterwards, she appeared to me in a vivid dream. She was helping me in a kitchen, which appeared to be mine. We were baking a roast meal, as well as lots of cakes etc. The cake tins and dishes were mine; they were the exact ones I still use. She was telling me that there was always plenty of food and she would keep helping me, especially in the kitchen. I knew without doubt that this was in fact a visitation from her because she absolutely loved baking, and she was an incredibly good cook!

I know with certainty that there is no such thing as death. Once the physical vehicle can no longer sustain us on the Earth plane of existence…either through illness or trauma, we simply leave it behind, and we take all the Love and all of our experiences with us when we leave… when we return to our true Home.

We live on in our Light Body.

That which has always been.

That which will always be.

That which is our natural state of existence.

CHAPTER THIRTEEN

Parental Love Ties

I know that my adored parents are not lost to me, and I know that I will be with them again when it is my time to return Home. I know that they are still alive and well, and living very happily with other family members and friends in a different dimension, or reality to this one. I know this because I see them and speak with them on a regular basis; however, this does not mean that I did not go through the loss and grief process...I did, and I still miss them beyond belief! I would much prefer that they were still here with me on the physical plane of existence, but having contact in this way does bring me great comfort.

I have had visitations with both of them, either separately or together, in a number of ways. I have met with them in dreams on the astral plane, as well as having met up with them in an altered state of consciousness, but I have also visited them at their home and at other places on the other side while I have been in an out of body state. They also visit me here to let me know that they are around me, especially at special times in my life, such as my birthday. It is my Mother who plays my music box for me!

These visits have been so comforting to me that I would like to share some of them with you, so you might gain an understanding of how this happens for me. I am sure that many of you have had similar experiences, and perhaps you have wondered whether it was real, or just an overactive imagination triggered by immense grief.

I am here to tell you that these visits are very real indeed. Please don't ever doubt that! As I have stated before, your Loved Ones live on, and they have taken the Love you share with them...that is never lost! Your adored pets also live on, and they love to visit you as well. I will share some of my visitations with mine in the next chapter.

My adored Dad made his transition to the other side on August 23rd 2000.

My darling Mum joined him there on May 2nd 2004.

On each of their birthdays and at Christmas time, as well as on the anniversaries of their wedding and their transitions, I light a candle for them.

I was given the understanding some time ago by Spirit that they are able to see a naked flame very easily, and they are drawn to it, rather than to an artificial light. I place a favorite photograph, as well as a small vase of flowers with the candle, and I just simply talk to them. At times during the conversation, the flame will dance and go crazy, even though there is not a breath of air, or any movement at all in the room. I believe that they are simply talking to me, and validating the fact that they are there with me.

I would encourage everyone to try it...simply open your mind and your heart, and observe what happens!

Journal: November 4th 2001

Early this morning, I found myself out of body, and I was with my Dad on the other side; I was hugging him, and also crying. He was a young man of about thirty, and he did not look as I knew him in this lifetime. He had similar coloring, but different facial features; even so, I knew that it was him. I had obviously surprised him, and he had not had the time to change his appearance, in order for me to see him. I had the rare privilege of seeing him in the body he prefers on the other side. He had long, dark, curly hair and a moustache, and he had his shirt off. He was using some kind of a hoe, and he was working in a large vegetable garden; the vegetables were very lush looking. He seemed really surprised to see me, and he told me that I was not supposed to be there, and I should go. I told him that I wanted to stay there with him, but he told me that I couldn't. He said that I would be there with him again soon enough and I must leave. I was crying, and then I found myself back in my body; I could not stop crying.

Note: My Dad loved his vegetable gardens in this lifetime too. Wherever we lived, he always provided us with a large assortment of fresh produce from his gardens.

Mostly, our departed Loved Ones will appear to us in the form we will recognize as them from this lifetime, but they can actually appear to us in any way they choose.

Journal: February 25th 2002

I came back to bed after heading to the bathroom about 4:30 a.m., and I was starting to doze off again when I saw Dad. He was a bit younger than when he passed; he was probably in his sixties, and he was sitting down. He still had both his legs, and he was dressed in one of his favorite outfits, which I instantly recognized. It was a pair of dark, tiny checked, long pants and a pinky brown, long sleeved shirt with flap over pockets on either side of the chest. He was very happy to see me, and I was very happy to see him. He only said one sentence to me, but I have no memory of what it was! I remember thinking that it wasn't anything really important, and perhaps that's why I haven't remembered it (I am pretty sure that it was some kind of a greeting), and then I went into a dreaming state. I know he was in the dream, but I can't remember what it was about; just that it didn't make much sense to me at the time.

Journal August 23rd 2002

I was dozing in bed early this morning when I felt a weight on my left shoulder. I was obviously slightly out of body, so I put my right hand up to my shoulder, and then I felt someone's forearm there. The next thing I knew, a hand closed over mine, and I recognized it as Dad's. He held his hand over mine for a moment, and then I became aware of a movement beside me.

I pulled my hand away to feel what it was, and I felt a skinny little leg! I realized that it could not have belonged to Dad, and then a laughing little voice said: Hello Nanna! I immediately recognized my Granddaughter's voice, and I said hello to her. I told her how wonderful it was to see her, and we started playing the tickling game we had made up between the two of us; she started giggling, and then she hopped onto my lap. She looked down at me with her lovely little face and her beautiful blonde hair, and I said: Come here you beautiful little thing, and lay your head on my shoulder...give your Nanna a great big hug and a kiss! She did, and the next thing I knew, one of my dogs was jumping up on the side of the bed to say good morning to me.

Note: It was the second anniversary of my Father's death, and I had asked him the night before if he could please visit me, or let me know in some way that he was around me. He not only did that, but he also brought me the most beautiful gift...a visit with my beloved Granddaughter, who only lived a couple of hours away from me at that time. Thank you Dad!

Journal: July 2nd 2004

I was dozing early this morning, and I was obviously

slightly out of body because I found myself with Mum and Dad. Mum was wearing a dress I remember well. She was talking to me exactly as she used to here. She spoke to me for a while, but I don't remember some of what she said. She said that she had told me she would still be here as part of our lives, and she had brought me a gift. She handed me a piece of pretty china. It was white with purple spots, and it was in the shape of what I thought was a Human head, but afterwards when I thought about it, I realized that it was some sort of a piggy bank. I thanked her, but told her that I couldn't take it because it wouldn't exist back here! She told me that it would remain with me, and then she stepped aside, and I saw Dad lying on the bed. I bent down to hug him and give him a kiss on the lips, and I remember asking myself if this was real or not. As that thought crossed my mind, he pressed his lips hard to mine. I actually felt the pressure from them, and I knew that it was real. They both disappeared, and when I came back into my body, I could still feel the pressure on my lips. The sensation remained for some time…it was definitely real!

Journal: August 7th 2004

I was drifting back to sleep early this morning when I became aware of watching my ex-husband and my older Daughter as she used to be when she was young. They appeared to be in the back yard of an old house, which we had owned when the girls were young, but it seemed to be a bit different. They were talking and laughing together, and then I found myself inside the house with my younger Daughter, who was a toddler. There didn't appear to be any furniture in the house; it was totally empty. My younger Daughter was running through the house, giggling like she used to do when she was that age; she was always a very happy little girl!

She ran into the main bedroom, and I followed her. I looked into the room, and on the far wall there was a white door where there had never been one before. There was a very bright light shining from around it. I went to open it, but instead of it opening out like a normal door, it dropped down on the floor in front of me. Mum was standing there in the bright Light! She was aged, but not as old and as sick looking as she had been just before she passed. She came towards me smiling, and we hugged. She spoke to me easily, and we were able to have a conversation as easily as if she was here with me now. Again, I asked her forgiveness for not being there with her when she "died." She just smiled and hugged me, and she said: I'll smack you on the "bumpty bum!" This was one of her sayings when she was here. She had often said it to me as an adult in a playful way if she thought that I had done something wrong. Just at that moment, my husband stirred beside me, and I was brought abruptly back into my body.

Journal: December 23rd 2005

Last night, I had a very vivid dream, which led to an O.B.E. I dreamt that I was sitting at a large table looking at some photos in an album. My friend was sitting beside me, and I was showing her some photos when I came across one of Mum. My friend looked up at me, and she asked me if I was alright because I had started to cry. I hardly heard her, and I remember saying: I Love you Mum, and I miss you terribly. Suddenly, I was aware that I was in my body in the bed, but in an altered state of consciousness, and I felt her hand touch mine. I grabbed onto her arm, and we clung together for some time as I felt her Love flowing through me. I feel that she was comforting me, as well as telling me that she was also giving me a bit of a helping hand.

Journal: June 20th 2006

I had a visit from Mum early this morning; she visited in a dream again. I was aware that I was dreaming, and I could see myself and my husband, as well as my Daughters and Granddaughters lying in my bed together, and then my consciousness moved into my body in the bed, and I looked up.

First of all, I just saw her legs dressed in tracksuit pants; she always wore a tracksuit! After a few moments, she appeared to me in her full form, and she looked like she did in her sixties with permed grey hair. I said: Mum is that really you? She said: Of course it is! For a moment, her facial appearance changed, and she looked old and sick, but then it changed back again. She started hugging and kissing us all. I remember thinking that the others probably couldn't see her, but then she bent down and put her arms around my husband's neck and kissed him on the cheek. He looked straight at her, and then he kissed her back. I spoke with her, and I had to focus really hard because I felt that I was losing the connection with her. I asked her if she visited us often. She replied that she did, and she was with me most of the time. She said: I told you that I would be. I could feel myself waking up, and I felt very emotional; I knew that I had definitely been with her.

Journal: January 15ᵗʰ 2008

I had a visit from Mum early this morning while I was in an altered state. I became aware of her and Dad having some sort of conversation about a car, and then I felt her close to me. I could even smell her scent, and then I could see her. I didn't see Dad, but I could sense his presence close by. I tried to lift my left arm to roll over and hug her properly, but I couldn't lift it. Then I realized that my younger Granddaughter was there as well, and she had her head resting on my arm! She moved, and I hugged Mum and told her how wonderful it was to see her and feel her again; I felt ecstatic. She told me again that she was always with me, just like she said she would be. I can't remember the rest, but I know that we spoke for a while. I am feeling much better after this encounter because I have been missing them both terribly lately.

Journal: April 16th 2009 (My 57th Birthday)

I had gone back to sleep early this morning, or at least I had tried to. Instead, I found myself inside a house, which seemed familiar to me. I was gliding, or hovering above the floor a few inches; it was almost like skating - one leg after the other. I have memories of moving like this before while I have been on the other side. I was searching each room, but they were all empty; they were furnished, but there was nobody in them. I reached the end of the hallway and entered the last room; this one had very little furniture in it, but there was a lovely rug on the floor. I looked across towards an alcove at the far end of the room, and there was Mum! She had her back to me, and for some reason I thought that maybe she would not be able to see me; I thought that there was some sort of veil dividing us. I went up to her, and I realized that I could hug her from behind. She turned around to me and hugged me back. I felt such Love and happiness. She looked me straight in the eyes, and said: One day you will be here with me and your Dad in The Kingdom of God! I don't remember anything more. When I came back, I could still feel her presence. What a beautiful birthday gift to me…it has stayed with me all day.

I had asked her for a birthday visit, and she delivered beautifully!

Journal: May 27th 2009

Early this morning, I had a very vivid dream; I was in some sort of hut. I think my younger Daughter was there as a child, and I was trying to sleep, but I was disturbed by an older woman, who came into the hut with a watering can to water the potted plants, which were lined up along one wall. I told her that it probably wasn't a good time to water the plants because it was night time, and she was disturbing us. She looked at me and walked over to where I was lying, and then she deliberately poured the water all over my back. I jumped from the dreaming state, and then found myself consciously aware on the other side; this often happens to me. I was walking towards a house, which I recognized as my Mother's. It was a brick house, and it resembled the kind of house my parents chose to live in during their lifetime here.

I was just about to knock on the door when it opened, and I was greeted by my Mother. She appeared younger with her dark hair and glasses, and she wore her Guide Leader's uniform. As I went past her into the living room,

I noticed a group of young girls sitting around on the floor. They appeared to be of different nationalities, and they were all talking, as well as doing things. They were obviously learning something, and they were being helped by a couple of older women, who were also dressed in uniforms. I walked past them all, but none of them seemed disturbed by me; it was almost as if they couldn't see me.

I asked Mum where Dad was, and she pointed to an area towards the end of the house. She told me to follow the house around, and then to go through the walkway. As I went further around, I came to a large glass door opening to the outside. I stopped and looked out; there was a beautiful grassed and paved courtyard with a small waterfall feature, and beautiful flowers and shrubs. Reclining on the grassed area were three gorgeous cats. One of them I recognized, but I didn't know the other two. I kept walking, and I eventually came to a small walkway, which took me into another section of the house; it was like a separate house, but it was attached to the other one.

I found Dad there and greeted him, but I got the distinct impression from him that I had surprised him, and I really shouldn't have been there. I remembered that my mother had seemed surprised to see me too. He was standing near some plants, and there were lots of potted plants and flowers everywhere. He seemed to be working with them and studying them somehow. I looked up at the ceiling, and there appeared to be some sort of paper lining covering it. I asked him if it was paper, but he said that it was some sort of material. He named it, but I had never heard of it, and I don't remember what it was now; although I do remember that it was a reddish pink color with white on it. I asked him why it was there, and he told me that it helped him with the acoustics for the plants. I don't remember anymore because I suddenly found myself visiting with my older Daughter in her home on the other side.

Note: My mother was involved in the Guiding Movement for most of her life. She had been a Brown Owl for many years before becoming a Guider Trainer. My Father always maintained the most beautiful gardens in all their homes. They both loved plants and gardening, and they passed that Love on to me and both my girls. It is when I am in my garden that I feel closest to them; I know that they are there with me!

Journal: September 24ᵗʰ 2010

I was with Mum early this morning at her lovely brick house on the other side. We were outside, and I was helping her water all these beautiful plants. Some were in hanging baskets, and there were a lot of wooden walkways and paths. As I drifted off to sleep last night, I asked my Angels to please help me to visit her house again, and to help me bring back the memory of it; they did!

I have deliberately left one of the first visitations my Father ever made to me as the last one in this chapter. This is because it was very special. It also involved a visitation by one of my much loved and much missed pets. Ralph was really my husband's pet...that dog lived for him alone! The Love they shared was really something to behold. We lost our gorgeous boy in January 2001 in very sad and tragic circumstances. He was deliberately poisoned by a vindictive, so called neighbor as a cowardly act of vengeance towards us for some imagined wrongdoing. He was only six years old, and Dad had loved him too. When Dad visited us at our property, Ralph would sit at his feet the whole time.

His loss still affects us in a profound way.

Journal: February 2nd, 2001

I had a lucid dream last night; Ralph met me in our hallway, and I was overjoyed to see him. I was extremely upset about him last night, and I was wishing that I could just cuddle him one last time. I bent down to cuddle him, and he wrapped his paws around my arms like he used to do, and then he cuddled me back. I was so happy, and it was so real that I yelled out to my husband that Ralph was back, and to come and see him quickly before he disappeared, but of course he couldn't hear me. I eventually realized that Ralph was not going to go, and he was staying right there with me. I was overjoyed, and I felt tremendous Love between us. I believe that this was a special visitation, and he was giving me that last cuddle I had been wishing for. As I felt his bristly hair against my face, I realized that I was actually out of body, and I was even aware of his smell. I know Dad must have helped him to come to me, but he must be a highly evolved Soul to be able to visit in that way.

As I came from the hallway with Ralph, I saw Dad sitting at my dining room table, and I went up to him and gave him a kiss and a hug. For some reason I realized that it was his birthday soon, so I wished him a happy birthday. He thanked me, and then he said that Mum hadn't given him her present yet. I can't remember anymore, but when I woke up this morning, I felt extremely emotional.

Note: My Dad always shared the same Love for our animal companions as I do, and it brings me great comfort to know that he is with my adored pets on the other side, helping to care for them until my return Home.

CHAPTER FOURTEEN
Our Beloved Pet Connections

Throughout my life, I have enjoyed a very special connection with our animal kingdom. Right from a very young age, I could tune into their emotions and sense the Love and devotion they so obviously felt for their Human companions. In my case that Love has always been reciprocated, and always will be. I believe that they incarnate with us on this planet as a selfless act of service to Humanity. They are here with us for two reasons: Healing and Unconditional Love...as simple as that!

I will never understand how any Human being can be capable of treating these trusting and loving Beings with such disrespect and downright cruelty, but I guess that says a lot about the people perpetrating these heinous acts doesn't it? If somebody can't love a beautiful, inoffensive animal, how can they ever truly Love another Human Being?

All animals have a Soul, or a Light Body...just as we do. Many people believe them to be inferior to us because they cannot talk, (they actually don't need to!) and therefore regard them as more lowly evolved than Humans, and of lower intelligence. Anyone who has ever been closely involved with an animal would not agree with this judgment. In fact, I believe it to be quite the opposite! I believe that animals are actually more evolved than most Human Beings because they act on instinct, and they remain connected to the natural world around them in a conscious way. They do not perceive themselves as being separate from The Source; they know no other way of being, and they know and understand a higher Truth than most Humans! I also believe that they don't need to reincarnate in quite the same way we do. They have no need to; they actually have nothing to learn!

We had a cat and a dog, and numerous birds and chickens when I was growing up, but as soon as I was old enough, I started to collect my own array of pets. Strangely enough, most of them found me…I did not go looking for them. The largest number of domestic pets I have ever accumulated at any given time is ten! We lived on a rural property for many years, so it was relatively easy to do, and when we made our move to Tasmania, we brought the remaining nine with us! Most of them have lived very long lives, and we have only ever lost a couple of them under the age of twelve. Sadly, five years on, only five of them remain, and three of those are very old...soon we will be down to two.

At this point in time, we do not intend to welcome any more into our lives...for a while anyway. When the older ones have gone home, it is our intention to travel our beautiful country. Hopefully our two younger dogs will still be with us, and they will be our travel companions. They are like our children, and we simply could not bear to be parted from them!

Sadly, on occasion, we have had to help our dear friends to go Home. We could not see them reach a point of suffering, and there have been quite a few heartbreaking vet visits over the years. The pain of doing this has been unbearable, but I know that they understood that we always acted from a place of Love. In fact, I believe that some of them may have actually been telling me: It's time now Mum!

When our beloved animal companions make their final trip home, (they actually exist between the two worlds while they are here) they remain connected to us in the same way as our Human Loved Ones do...through Love! They also visit us often, just to let us know that they haven't really left us. They also like to revisit their favorite places...a favorite spot in the sun perhaps, or curl up next to the fire like one of my cats does regularly!

Kitty, (the children's name for him when he came to us as a kitten) or Harold as my husband renamed him (I have absolutely no idea why...he always answered to both names!) was our oldest cat, and along with all the others, he made the long trip to our new home with us. We weren't sure if he would make it because he was sixteen at the time, and he was not in the best of health. Sadly, he did not survive the first winter, and we found him one morning curled up in his basket; he had passed over very peacefully. Before he left us, his favorite place in his new world was in the living room directly in front of the fireplace. Sometimes, when the fire is burning brightly, we can still catch a glimpse of him there.

We found out sometime after he had gone that the couple who lovingly cared for this house for over half a century, and raised their family here were named Kitty and Harold, so there you are!

Our lives seem to be interwoven with many such strange coincidences. There's that word again! I prefer to call it synchronicity.

I must also point out here that not only are we visited by the pets we have been with during this lifetime, but we are also visited by our animal companions from our many past lifetimes.

Journal: December 12th 1999

As I was drifting off to sleep last night, I was disturbed by a weight jumping onto the side of the bed. I felt something settling down around my curled up legs, so I half sat up, and I could feel the fur of a cat. I assumed that Kitty had been inadvertently left inside, so I decided to go back to sleep. After a while, I felt him move again, so I sat up and gave him a pat around the ears. He stood up and walked over to my husband's side of the bed. Shortly afterwards, I heard a cat crying; I thought that the sound was coming from the verandah. I assumed that it was one of my other cats, so I got up and opened the front door to let it in, but there was no cat there.

My husband was disturbed by me opening the door, and he spoke to me. I asked him if he had left Kitty inside, but he said that he had put him outside before we went to bed. When I woke up the next morning, all our cats were outside waiting to be let in. I realized then that I must have had a visit from my old deceased cat, Moggy. There were definitely no living cats inside the house during the night.

Note: This was not the first time I have had a visit from Moggy. He came into our lives as a kitten at almost the same time my younger daughter was born. They grew up together, but sadly, he did not quite make their seventeenth birthday. She had never known a time without him as a part of her life, and it was heartbreaking for all of us.

A few weeks after he had gone Home to the other side, I had a visit from him. I was lying in bed almost asleep one night when I heard a very loud noise…like static on a radio. Next thing I knew, Moggy was rubbing himself up against my arm and purring. I was aware of him standing on my chest and looking directly into my eyes; however, he had not come alone; he had brought a couple of friends with him! To my utter amazement, I became aware of a large cow and a magnificent lion standing with him!

I put my hand out to stroke the lion, and he took my hand in his mouth and bit down hard. Out of body or not, I can tell you, I was gripped with intense pain! I looked him straight in the eyes, and I told him that he did not have to be aggressive like that anymore because there was absolutely nothing that could hurt him now. He immediately dropped my hand, and then he allowed me to stroke his face. I have never felt anything as smooth and as silky as that face…it was like velvet, and I feel incredibly privileged to have experienced such a close and personal encounter with such a magnificent animal.

Journal: January 1st 2001

As I was drifting off to sleep last night, I felt the movement of a cat to my side; all my cats were outside. I was aware of the fact that I was slightly out of body, and as I reached over to cuddle it, I was astounded to find one to the left of me, and two more to the right…three in all! I cuddled them all, and then happily drifted off to sleep.

Journal: April 9th 2001

Sometime during the night, I became aware of a weight on top of my body. I was lying on my side, and as I lifted my right hand to feel what it was, I became aware of a number of cats with me again; there were four of them this time. One was striped like Buffy, but this one had more ginger in the coloring. Another one had white on it, and the others were black. They were all snuggled right into my body. I noticed that Buffy was still sleeping at the bottom of the bed. She was the only cat inside for the night...in a physical sense anyway!

Note: Buffy was a very special cat. If it is at all possible to Love one more than the others, then she was it...for me anyway...more about her later!

While my daughters were growing up, we also shared our lives with an adorable female boxer dog called Patches. She was twelve and a half years old when she passed, and unfortunately it was one of those heartbreaking times when we had to make the call and take her to the vet one last time. Afterwards, I played it out in my mind over and over, and cried over it constantly; I just couldn't seem to get past it. Even though I knew that her body had been racked with cancer, and we had done the best thing possible for her, I still worried that we had sent her home too soon.

Although I had caught a few glimpses of her coming out of our garage where her favorite lounge chair had been set up for her previously, this was her first visit to me, and it came just over a year after she had passed.

Journal: October 1st 2001

After my husband had left the room this morning, I went back to sleep, and I had a lucid dream with Patches in it. We were near some sort of water, and she was young again and running free. Every time I saw her, she was with Bobby…another of our dogs; he was there too! I was so happy to see her that I ran up to her. She rolled onto her back at my feet, and I bent down and hugged and cuddled her. I could feel the bristly fur around her neck against my face, and then I noticed that her eyes were closed, which I thought was rather strange.

For some reason, it seemed important to me that I see her with her eyes open, and for me to look into them. I think that it was because I still hold the vision of her at the moment of her passing. Her eyes remained open, but there was nothing there. They were empty without the Light of her Soul shining from them, and it still haunts me.

I opened her eyes with my hands, and they were shining with a pale golden light! I got a bit of a shock, but she was looking at me with such Love that I knew it was a visitation from her, and something very special. She was showing me the Soul Light in her eyes that I had seen as missing when she passed; she was showing me that she was still there.

I woke up with tears on my face.

Note: There are tears on my face now as I write this. She will be forever loved and sadly missed, but I know that she lives on, happy on the other side, waiting with all the others for me to return home. What a wonderful re-union that will be!

Journal: April 6th 2002

My beautiful cats again! I was lying half-awake early this morning when I felt movement on the bed. Whatever it was moved up around my head, and it pulled my hair slightly as it stood there. I became aware of movement all around me, and then I felt a heavy thump on the bed beside me. I realized at this point that I was out of body, so I lifted my arms and felt around me; there were at least five cats with me. I held out my arms, and I lifted one of them towards me and gave it a cuddle; they were all different colors. I can't remember all of them, but there was a ginger one and a very large one, which was totally black with white markings on its face!

While we were living at our rural property in

Queensland, our larger dogs were always housed in the garage at night, rather than in the house because they were also our guard dogs. The following account is of a visitation by one of my dogs. Bobby was still very much alive, but asleep in his bed in our garage. A living animal can very obviously visit in its Light Body too, just as Humans do!

Journal: February 11ᵗʰ 2003

During the night, I became aware of a movement and a presence beside the bed. I realized that I was out of body, and there was a large dog just sitting there, wagging its tail and looking at me. I put my hand over and patted him, and said: Oh, it's you mate, what are you doing here? It was Bobby! He was very obviously out of body also, and he had come to visit me. I felt his ears and his face, and then I gave him a hug.

Note: Although he is now aged, we are blessed to still have Bobby with us.

I have had a love affair with little Pekingese dogs ever since my husband at the time presented me with one for my twenty-first birthday. Her name was Lee-sing, and I was totally In Love with her. I had her for fifteen wonderful years. I also had a little male Peke called Chung. Sadly, unbeknown to us, he had been interbred, and he had inherited a genetic disorder, which unfortunately took him from us at the age of eight.

My last little Peke was called Sue-ling, but she was more affectionately known as Susie. I was blessed to have her for close to thirteen years, but towards the end of her time, her kidneys started to break down, and she became too sick to carry on. In consultation with our vet, it was decided that the best thing to do for her would be to send her Home to the other side. It was one of the saddest days of my life. As is usual in these situations, I stayed with her, and I held her and kissed her, and told her how much I loved her throughout the whole process. I also thanked her for being such a special part of our lives. She left us on February 11th 2004.

It never gets any easier.

Journal: March 11th 2004

I had a vivid dream with Susie in it this morning. It is exactly a month since we said our good-byes. I was in the house, and as I looked down at the floor, I saw her lying there. I was so happy to see her again, and I called out to my husband to come and see her. I bent down and picked her up, and she allowed me to kiss and cuddle her. She snuggled into me, but she did not open her eyes to look at me. She appeared to be younger, and she was not sick anymore. I believe that by not opening her eyes and looking at me, she was validating the fact that this was indeed a visitation from her. Just before I took her to the vet, she lay on the bed with me and gave me the biggest love and cuddle, and she stood straight up to my face and looked me directly in the eyes...she was telling me that she knew! I was also stunned to see that her eyes were a liquid black, just like they were when she was young. She had been almost blind for some time, and her eyes were usually opaque.

Now back to Buffy

This very special cat came to us in a very unusual manner. While living at our property, we had to dispose of our own rubbish. This required a regular run over rough, dirt roads to the rubbish tip, which was about ten kilometers away. One Sunday morning while my husband was doing this run, a kitten ran out in front of the car, and he thought that he had run over it, so he stopped to check to see if it was still alive. The rubbish tip was over-run with feral cats, and there were always plenty of them around that general vicinity. To his amazement, the kitten simply looked at him, and then curled up in his hand...she did not have a mark on her. He did not have the heart to leave her there, so he found an old small enamel saucepan at the tip, and placed her in it for the trip home, thinking that we might be able to find her a nice home somewhere.

When he arrived home, he presented me with the saucepan, which just happened to have a kitten's head poking out from the top! She was extremely malnourished, and she also had a dreadful smell to her, so the first thing I did was bathe her. She was probably about three months old at the time, but very small. I fell "In Love" with her, but I knew that I couldn't keep her because we already had four cats. I decided that I would keep her for a short time and try to build her health up a bit, and then I would take her to the local pet shop and try to find her a loving home.

The day came when I had to put her in the cage for the trip into town, but I could not stop crying. I got as far as outside the pet shop. I even took the cage out of the car, but I just could not do it; I simply loved her too much! She returned home with us, and we resigned ourselves to the fact that we had yet another mouth to feed!

Buffy came to Tasmania with us along with all the others, but she did not cope well. She was always very skittish, but the strange kennels and all the travel, including a long plane flight had obviously taken a huge toll on her. I kept all the cats inside their new home for the first week, and after this time the others were ready to go exploring, but not this girl! She remained glued to the chair at one of the front windows, and she would not venture outside at all.

Finally, after a few more days, just after we arrived home from dinner out at a local café, she went to the back door and asked to be let out. It was dark, and I was hesitant to do this, but she remained insistent. Finally I relented, and I went outside with her. She walked around for a bit, and then disappeared into the darkness. I called and called her, but I have never seen my gorgeous girl again...not in the flesh anyway. I remain absolutely heartbroken; she was eight years old. We searched for weeks, and we even put out calls over the local radio station, but to no avail. I believe that she was frightened by something, and she just took off and became lost. She must have been broken-hearted to have lost us also.

She disappeared in late February of 2006, and soon after that, she started communicating with me in dreams, and while I was in an altered state of consciousness. I believe that she was still alive while most of these communications were taking place.

The first time, she simply visited with me and let me cuddle her. I don't know whether it was to draw comfort from me, or to give me some measure of comfort; perhaps it was both. The second time, she began to show me what was happening to her; she showed herself to me standing on top of a pile of boxes. I appeared to be standing at the top of a staircase as I was observing this. It was so real; I thought she was really home with me. I grabbed for her, and I actually thought that I had her, but she pulled away from me as though she was trying to tell that me she wasn't ready yet, or she was simply unable to come home.

The third time was very upsetting. She appeared to have something wrong with her face, as if it was being eaten away by something. I cried and cried because I knew that something was dreadfully wrong with her, and I wasn't there to help her. I remembered that when she had her vet check before travelling, our vet had found a lump inside her mouth, which he was concerned about, and he told us to get it seen to when we found a new vet here; that of course had not been able to happen. The next time she appeared to me, she ran away from me, and then she disappeared down what appeared to be a rabbit hole.

The last time she appeared to me in this series of visits, she was young and beautiful, and she appeared to be whole again. She had finally gone Home to the other side, and she was telling me that she was safe and well at last. What an incredible communicator, and what an incredible bond of Love we share!

Journal: February 11th 2007

I was drifting off to sleep early this morning when I felt a thump on the end of the bed again. After a moment or two I felt a cat start to walk up the middle of my legs and onto my stomach. I became fully aware out of body and scratched it around the ears. It cuddled into me and started purring, and I felt tremendous Love coming from it. I thought it might be Buffy, but soon realized that it wasn't because it was Kitty! Suddenly, I felt another movement to the side of me, and as I reached over, I realized that Buffy was there also. I cuddled the two of them together, and I felt so happy! After a while I realized that there was a third cat present...a black one, but it didn't look like Moggy; I did not recognize this one. They all curled up into my body and slept soundly.

Note: I have had many other visitations from my cats. Most of them I do not recognize, but they are obviously connected to me with Love. I am assuming that we have shared our lives in the past, and they are some of the many waiting for me to return home. When that happens, I know that I will remember them, and we will recognize each other as though we have never been apart.

This Chapter would not be complete without mention of another one of our cats...Georgie. He was only a part of our lives for eighteen short months, but he managed to Love his way into our hearts in a big way. Strangely, or not so strangely, he arrived as a tiny kitten; he just appeared one morning in our front yard. His home could not be found, and he looked as though he had not eaten in a while, so we took him in and gave him a home. I am sure that he was delivered express post from the universe to alleviate some of the heartache of losing our beloved

Kitty. Would you believe that we lost Kitty just four days after Georgie`s arrival?

Of course you would!

Besides Buffy, this little cat was probably the most loving of them all. When he wanted something, he would come and stand near me and stretch out his front legs. He would then literally bow down on the floor while he let out a loud cry!

For some reason, I always knew that he was not going to be in our lives for long. He always slept inside in his basket with the two little dogs, but in summer he would often ask to be let out about five o'clock in the morning. He was always at the back door to be let back in to be fed when we got up a couple of hours later.

One morning, he did not respond to our calling, and we thought that something had happened to him. Three days later, he arrived home worse for wear, and it was very obvious that he had not eaten. We came to the conclusion that he must have been locked in a shed or something because he was always inquisitive and getting into places he shouldn't have been. A few weeks later he disappeared again, and we were hopeful that he would arrive home in a few days like the last time, but sadly, we have never seen him again.

Journal: December 9th 2008

I was dozing this morning, and I must have gone deeply into an altered state. When I was coming back, I remembered that I had seen my darling little Georgie. He saw me and approached me, and he stretched his whole body out in front of him, just like he used to do, and then he gave me his little "meow." I picked him up and gave him a big cuddle...I was so happy to see him!

Note: This is the only visit I have ever had from him, and I have not seen him with the other cats sleeping with me on my bed at night. I really don't know if he is still alive and happy in a new home somewhere (he was so friendly and would go up to anyone), and he just popped in for a visit, or whether he has gone Home to the other side. I have not seen him again, but I guess that either way, he has let me know that he is still alive and well!

Benny

Benny was a gorgeous, saddle-back roan cocker spaniel. He and I shared a very special bond, and it is still hard for me to talk about him. We took him for his final visit to the vet about eighteen months ago. Our vet assured us that it was the kindest thing to do for him under the circumstances. He was very old, and he had lost a lot of weight. We also knew that he was beginning to suffer with pain from his cancer. He slept most of the time, but when he wasn't, he would not leave my side. If he couldn't find me when he woke up, he would cry out for me, and it became very distressing for both of us. He was about fifteen years old when he passed. We weren't exactly sure of his age because we had rescued him from the R.S.P.C.A. ten years earlier, and they didn't really know his age at the time; their vet estimated that he was about four. The staff had come into work one morning to find him tied up to the fence with a piece of rope. When we found him, he was on death row…he actually only had one day's grace!

I have never been able to go into a dog pound. Because I feel what the animals are feeling, I find it far too distressing. Believe me when I say that they know exactly what is going on! We had actually enquired about a dog they had advertised in the paper, but he had already found a home; however, they asked us if we would please consider taking Benny…the staff had already named him. They were very fond of him, and were extremely distressed about the fact that he was going to have to be put down the next day.

My husband decided that he should at least take a look at him…always a mistake! Once seen, there was no way he was going to leave him there was there? I stayed in the car while he checked him out. Apparently Benny just went crazy over him, and the moment my husband saw him, he knew that I would Love him. I grew up with a black cocker spaniel, which had belonged to dear friends of our family, and I have always loved the breed, even though they can be quite crazy at times!

We had to leave him there while we went to the bank to get the money to pay for him. While that was happening, they were going to give him a bath. He had started to howl the moment my husband had walked away from him. We could still hear him as we drove away, and apparently he did not stop until he saw my husband appear again. When he was ready, the girl brought him outside on a lead. She told us that he was still a bit damp, so it would be best to put an old towel on the back seat for him. Benny had other ideas! He looked over at the car and spotted me in the passenger seat with the door open, and there was no stopping him! He pulled the lead out of her hand, bounced through the dirt, and jumped straight into the car and onto my lap. He then proceeded to deliver the biggest doggy kisses to my face, as though he knew me, but had not seen me in a long while. I was wearing good clothes, and I was soaked and dirty from him, but somehow, I just did not mind at all. I was totally "In Love"…again!

When we arrived home, I opened the car door to let him out, but instead of waiting for me to put his lead on, he headed straight out the door and came face to face with Buffy; she had obviously been watching the proceedings from under a bush at the back door. She swiped his nose in fright, and he chased her up a large gum tree! It took us a full day to finally coax her down. A full year of confrontation between the two of them ensued, and it almost drove me insane! I had to literally keep them separated at all times.

What we didn't realize when we got him was that he was a runner! We had no proper fencing around the property either; we only had barbed wire. After retrieving him a few times from neighboring properties, we finally had to restrain him by keeping him inside, or on a run outside. He also loved to sit tied up to the park bench on the verandah where he could watch all the outdoor activity.

When he was inside the house, we could not go in or out the front or back doors without watching him because he would make a run for it! It was impossible to stop him because he was so strong, and so fast! Each time he managed to escape, the only way we could coax him home was to drive the car down to the bottom paddock, and then call him with the car door left open. Eventually, he would come and just jump into the car, as though it was his royal right to be chauffeured home! One day, after we had him for a year or so, he made yet another escape. We eventually retrieved him, but this time his whole coat was full of grass seed. I had finally had enough, and while I was cutting the seeds out of his hair, (this took at least an hour) I was berating him, and telling him that I was going to send him back to the pound!

Of course I didn't, but the strangest thing happened…he and Buffy never had another confrontation. Peace reigned supreme between them from that moment on; however, he still managed to escape from time to time! When we moved to Tasmania, we made sure that we bought a house with a large, fully fenced yard. He spent the last years of his life running freely on his half acre, and it was the most beautiful thing to behold. Even when his sight dimmed and he was almost blind, he would still do his run around the perimeter of the property at least twice a day; he loved it here! We said our final good-byes on December 10th 2009, and it literally broke our hearts.

Journal: January 24th 2010

I had an early morning visit with my darling Benny. I found myself in my house on the other side, and as I walked down the stairs from the verandah, I saw Chloe and Toto lying there. I walked along the path towards the front gate, and as I looked up, I noticed a number of dogs to my right. Two of them obviously knew me, and they came up to me for a love and a cuddle. One was a beautiful black Labrador, and the other one was a big dog with a shaggy, red-brown coat. I knew them at the time, but I don't now; they were obviously from times past! Out of the corner of my eye, I saw Benny appear. He disappeared for a moment, and then he reappeared up closer to me. He came over to me, and we just loved each other! He looked into my eyes while I rubbed his ears and down his neck; he always loved me to do that! Just to reassure myself that this was real, I put my face to his, and I smelled him and kissed him.

We hugged for ages, and then I found myself back on the verandah of my house. It is a very wide, wooden verandah, and there are big, wide, wood and glass French doors leading inside into the living room. There are white sheer curtains at the side of each door, and they were billowing gently in a soft breeze. I found myself talking to a woman, who called herself Deidre. She had short, dark hair, and she was asking me if I would be prepared to travel with my spiritual work. I told her that I would be happy to do that if it was not too far afield; I don't remember anymore.

Note: I now think I may have heard this name incorrectly…I think it was in fact, Didi.

This meeting took place a couple of months before she made herself known to me on a conscious level.

Chloe and Toto are my two little dogs. I still have them here with me, so I guess that they must accompany me at night when I travel to my "other" house!

I have only seen Benny on one other occasion. It was in the form of a vision, which he used as a means of communication. I was relaxing down one night ready for sleep, and as is often the case, I started thinking about my beautiful pets. We had left Benny with the vet to be buried; we have done this with all our dogs. The vet had described the beautiful place where this would take place, and as I started to wonder about it, Benny suddenly appeared to me through my third eye vision. He showed himself to me side-on with his head down and his bum up in a field of bright green grass, which came half way up his side. He still had his beautiful golden colored curls, and his head was so far down that it was mostly covered by his big, floppy ears. I believe that he was telling me not to wonder where his physical body was because it didn't really matter. He wanted me to see him where he is now, happily playing in a field of lush green!

We have had to say good-bye to one more of our dear pets since Benny passed. One of our black cats we named Fred went Home a year ago. He left us in February 2010. He was the most placid of all our cats, and in fact, he was the one we chose to keep from a litter of five; our two older black cats had managed to mate before we had them de-sexed. Although they are now aged, we still have his mother and his father, so a part of him is still with us… for the time being at least!

I have visited with Freddie only once, and that was at my house on the other side, so I know that he is there waiting for me; it was soon after he passed. Again, as I walked out to my front gate, I became aware of Buffy standing over to my right. As I bent down to greet and cuddle her, I looked over further, and Fred was sitting there with his big black fluffy tail curled around him, just like it always was here.

He made no attempt to come to me, but he watched my every move with Buffy. For some reason, I knew not to approach him. He was obviously not ready to greet me yet, but I know that he will be some day...when he is ready.

I look forward to that moment with great anticipation!

I would like to end this chapter with one more very special animal visitation. I have no idea where this gorgeous dog fits into my many lifetimes, but I know with certainty that he has a very strong connection with me still. He decided to pay me a visit fairly recently, and I can honestly say that even with all my other animal visitations, this one has been by far the strongest. It took place in my bedroom, and even now I have absolute, complete memory of it. I can recall every little physical detail about him. During this out of body visitation, I experienced what I can only describe as a state of pure "bliss."

Journal: November 12ᵗʰ 2010

Early this morning, after my husband had left the bedroom and closed the door behind him, I felt myself moving very quickly into an altered state of consciousness. I heard what I thought was someone coming into the room again, and then land heavily onto the bed beside me, ruffling the bedcovers up as they did so. I thought that my husband must have decided to come back to bed, so I brought myself back and opened my eyes, but when I looked, there was nobody there. I immediately drifted back into my altered state, and when I felt around me on the bed, I became aware of a dog sitting beside me. I thought Benny must have come for a visit, and I felt so happy. I reached out to feel his floppy ears, but I was amazed to find that this dog's ears were short and slightly folded over. I consciously opened my spirit eyes, and I found myself looking directly into the eyes of one of the most gorgeous dogs I have ever encountered.

I haven't known him in this lifetime, but I knew that he had been with me in the past. For some reason, he reminded me of an old fashioned England or France. I consciously left my body and sat with him on the bed in my Light Body, and I played with him and cuddled him for what seemed like ages. I was absolutely ecstatic, and I was totally filled with Love for him. I was so excited that I didn't even think to ask him his name. I told him how happy I was that he had visited me, and he made a very happy, contented, low growling noise as he stared straight into my eyes.

He was of medium to large size, and he had longer hair on his long tail, but his main coat was fairly short. His predominant color was white with black markings all through it…like fine dots, but these dots appeared more speckled than solid. We must have spent about twenty minutes together, and then I was brought back with the sound of my husband bringing my breakfast into me. I could still smell him and feel his breath on my cheek while I was having my breakfast; I could not stop smiling all day.

An absolutely, unforgettable experience!

Note: Later in the day, I was berating myself about not asking him his name when I heard Antoine's voice saying: ***Tamblyn! - Tam for short; you used to call him Tam!***

I thought Tamblyn was a female name, so I looked up the meaning, and it very definitely is a male name, although it is my understanding that it is also popular now as a female name.

When used as a surname, Tamblyn is of English origin.

CHAPTER FIFTEEN

A Message Of Comfort And Support

As I have been writing the preceding chapter, two things have been happening.

The first: I was becoming increasingly concerned because there was so much that I wanted to include, I thought perhaps you might become bored while reading it. I felt that two consecutive chapters sharing my spiritual visitations with my Loved Ones (Human and Animal) were possibly too much, but Antoine and Lightcrow were insistent that it was to be done this way. Without any clear understanding of why this was, I did as they asked of me. If there is one thing I have learned to do, it is to trust them, and this process.

The second: The Japanese earthquakes and tsunami.

I now understand.

I think you will too.

This morning, I received the following channel from Antoine, which he has asked me to share with you. This was quickly followed by one from Lightcrow.

The first part from Lightcrow was for me personally,

which I feel compelled to share with you, while the second part is for anyone who might wish to hear the words.

Thursday March 17th 2011

Antoine

If there is one message that we would repeat over and over again to Humanity at this time, it is this:

"When your physical body can no longer sustain life in a physical sense...no matter what the circumstances...you do not just stop existing! You live on in your Light Body...your natural state of existence, and you return to your real Home in the higher dimensions of consciousness. It is just like walking through an open door from one room into another, and you have all done it many times before. It is a natural thing for you to do. There is nothing to be afraid of! There are many here, who would welcome your arrival with great joy...just as there are many there, who would mourn your departure. You will all understand this eventually, but there are those on your planet at this moment in your time, who already understand this concept, through the vehicle of their own higher, spiritual experiences. These we would seek to employ at this time as our messengers."

Antoine

We would also ask of you Child: "Please continue to spread this message through our words, and through the words of your own Truth, as far and as wide as possible. It is now becoming increasingly important that as many people as possible consciously remember and understand this simple Truth."

Lightcrow

Dear one,

We understand that you have recently experienced some *un-pleasant-ness* caused by passing our message on to someone who did not hear.

This *un-conscious-ness* you have recently witnessed is widespread throughout the majority of Human Beings on your planet. They remain attached to their fears and life dramas, and they do not see what is in front of their eyes. They do not want to see, but soon they will have to see! Soon they will seek to hear our message because soon nobody on your planet will be able to deny the fact that something very profound and unusual is taking place throughout your world at this time.

This is not an easy task you have undertaken Beloved. You may encounter this reaction again, but we ask you not to step back from your Truth; indeed, from our Truth. We would ask you instead to transmute the negative energy from that experience into positive energy, and use it as a catalyst to move further forward on your journey. Simply move away from the situation as you have done, and keep walking forward with your head held high, and your Light shining brightly for all to see. Time moves forward very quickly now, and many will be seeking that Light. Dear One, we ask you to walk as one with us and continue to hear our words; indeed, continue to write our words.

Note: I recently commented on a "friend's" status on a popular social site. This person had obviously entered into a place of fear with what was happening in the world at the moment. She seemed to think that Mother Earth was angry at us about something, and that this was a form of retribution towards Humanity. She was spreading that message to all of her "friends," and I felt that the space had been created for me to offer a few words of what I thought was comfort about the loss of life, and a short account of what was really happening. There was no response from her, and for someone who always commented on everything, that spoke volumes to me; however, the attack towards me by one of her "friends" was swift and totally unwarranted. This person had obviously not understood a word of what I had said, but was quick to make personal comments and judgments about me anyway.

My reaction was to immediately retract my comment, so as not to upset anyone further, and to delete my "friend" from my friend's list. This was not done in anger, or for vengeance…it was simply done so that I could walk away from the situation. I understand that they were obviously not ready to hear the message, and I make absolutely no judgment about that because that is their choice, but I do feel that the personal attack was uncalled for, and I will admit that it threw me off balance for a short time. It is never my intention to upset anyone; in fact, my intention is always quite the opposite!

I understood when I agreed to do this work that I would be opening myself up to ridicule. I also understood that this work was too important to allow that to influence my decision; however, I refuse to be drawn into, or enter into a place of conflict.

Lightcrow

Greetings Dear Ones,

Heartache and still more heartache, this is what we are witnessing on your planet from our vantage point. We say to you now with Love in our hearts: We feel your pain; we understand your pain. We tell you now that there are two sides to this story; two points of perspective from which to look at this situation. It is entirely your choice from which point you choose to view your current world events, but we would offer you some understanding of the situation from our perspective.

The many who have returned Home to us indeed feel sadness for the Loved Ones they have left behind, and for the pain and suffering many are experiencing, but they are also at peace, and are joyous and happy to be Home again. They are content in the knowledge that they have played their part in this process so well. They watch in wonder as they observe the many peoples of your world unite in one giant humanitarian effort. This connection of the Human family has been one of the desired outcomes... one side of the coin so to speak, in your world of duality. The other side is the necessary process of cleansing the Earth's energy grid.

The people who have returned Home during this important process have successfully completed their contract...the very reason for their incarnation. It would do well to remember that this has been their choice. This is hard for many of you to hear right now, especially when you bear witness to so much Human suffering, but we tell you now that this is indeed a higher Truth.

Through their sacrifice, and this is only your Human term because they do not see it that way, much good comes. During what you would term natural disasters, people are drawn together in a profound way. When there has been destruction and loss of Human life on a large scale, not only are larger numbers of people drawn into the web of the connection vibration, but those affected first hand...the survivors if you like are drawn together in a new way; they connect with a new level of understanding. This produces what you would term a domino effect throughout your world. We know many of you will not understand it in this way as yet, but we say to you that this is also the concept of a higher Truth that we offer you.

All of you are playing your part in this process of evolution...you have all chosen this! You chose to evolve to a higher level of consciousness while still inhabiting your planet, and you agreed to this process in a wonderful act of co-creation with Mother Earth and her helpers. Long before you incarnated on your planet this has been your destiny...your choice. You could have chosen to allow your world to end... just as many who do not understand what is happening are predicting will happen, but instead you chose a new cycle of evolution. To facilitate this process, these changes must take place, and indeed, it is the only way the desired outcome is possible. You all know this; you just have to remember it.

You must remember it!

We tell you now that your world is not going to end. Please do not be alarmed...do not be afraid! You are simply entering a New Age...a new way of interacting with each other, as well as with the planet which sustains you. You are creating a New World...one where Peace and Unconditional Love will reign!

Everything that is occurring on your world is in perfect harmony with All That Is. We understand that these words are hard to hear, or to understand for many of you right now, but we would tell you again that you are indeed creating Heaven on Earth!

We have told you before of the energetic fields and grids within Mother Earth; these hold much old and dense energy. We say to you now: There are some areas on your planet holding much more of these energies than others, and these areas require stronger cleansing. One of these areas you refer to as The Pacific Rim. You might think that much of the energy in this area was accumulated and embedded during what you would term your wartime. This is one piece of the story, but we tell you now that what you refer to as the Pacific is simply an energy portal. There are still places throughout this area where these changes will take place. We want you to understand that this is in no way an act of retribution by Mother Earth, or the universe, nor is it what you would term Karma. This is simply an agreed act of co-creation between Humanity and Mother Earth and Her helpers.

This clearing out has to take place before the new waves of energy needed to sustain your New World can be embedded, and they are indeed arriving at an ever increasing pace. These new energies are very strong and much lighter, and they vibrate at a much higher frequency. They are affecting, and will continue to affect you and everything on your planet in many ways, including your way of thinking and your way of being. They will also affect your concept of time as you understand it.

As these changes take effect, you will also experience more unrest in many areas of your planet as people rise up to regain their personal power. This will happen on an individual basis, as well as on a much larger global scale. The new, higher frequency energies will simply no longer support control and oppression by individuals, or government or religious regimes. That time is now finished...the Truth will be told!

Some of these world events will also impact on your economy, and they will help facilitate the necessary change from a world economy based on money to one based on Unconditional Love. You can see how this will work perhaps? It is time now for a new way of thinking; indeed, a new gentler way of being; a time for compassion, and a time for Unconditional Love towards Mother Earth and towards each other!

The people of the Japans have always maintained an innate understanding of who they truly are; they have also maintained their connection to Spirit, and those who have returned Home to us would now offer you these words of comfort:

"Please do not shed tears for us, for we are happy and at peace. We have completed our task of helping to unite Humanity. Instead, we would ask you to send much Love and

Light to those still completing this important process. We did not suffer in any way; in fact, we consciously walked peacefully through the opened doors before that point could be reached. There were many beings of Light, who had gathered to help us. We were ready! We understood that it was our time to return Home. Be assured that we still live on, and now we help you from these higher dimensions of reality; we also offer you our continued Love and support."

CHAPTER SIXTEEN

Discernment

I was sitting at my desk, contemplating writing the next chapter, and I had just made the decision to share some more of my visions and experiences with you… the ones that have delivered specific guidance to me in certain situations when I have needed it most, but unexpectedly, I heard Lightcrow speak to me. I was quite surprised to say the least because it was about a subject, which quite honestly, I have never given much thought to. I have always simply accepted my own guidance as my Truth…in whichever way it has been presented to me. I have always sensed and known that the source has been from the Light, but it would seem that this is not always the case for everyone, especially at this time, and we need to be consciously aware of this.

Lightcrow

We would ask something of you Dear one: Before you write your words concerning your own guidance, would you perhaps allow us to offer our words concerning the concept of Discernment? This is particularly relevant to your world at this time, and we would like to offer an understanding to all as to why this is so.

Greetings Dear Ones,

We welcome you into our circle once again, and we say to you now with Love in our hearts: More and more is being revealed to you, not only on a conscious level, but also on a subconscious level. Some of this information might appear confusing to you, and we tell you that this may be because it is not always what it appears to be. Unfortunately, not all information, or guidance that Humanity might receive, whether first hand or second hand, and from all planes of existence is actually infused with the pure Light of Love; indeed, sometimes it may be very deceptive! We tell you now that there are those who would not want this shift in consciousness to take place.

All Light must have a shadow, and it is this shadow, which would try to prevent this process from taking place because it has its own agenda; indeed, it does not want the Truth to be told. It does not want our message to be heard, and it will try anything to prevent that from happening. It cannot however, stop this shift from occurring because it is already in place...already begun in a profound way. It will happen! Have no fear of that Dear Ones, but those who would try to prevent it will keep trying anyway, simply to cause confusion and fear. The shadow thrives on this negative energy…it feeds on this energy! It does not want you to know who you truly are. You would then recognize your own power, and that would not serve its agenda at all!

All Humans are blessed with the innate ability to discern whether something is Truth or not. Take only that which is Truth for you Dear Ones…take only that which resonates with the vibration of your own Soul, and simply leave the rest! You have a feeling, or a knowing that something is not right for you. This is your intuition, and we would ask you to be consciously aware of this now, and to practice it with everything…absolutely everything! This is of the utmost importance! Some of the information filtering through to Humanity at this time may appear to emanate from the Light, but it may in fact only be a deception to try to fool you. It may emanate from the shadow, and simply be cleverly disguised as the Light. Some of the messengers themselves may merely be shrouded in a cloak of false Light. You must learn to be discerning with these messages, and listen with your heart instead of your mind; indeed, listen with your Soul!

We are many from The One...The One Consciousness of pure Light and Love, who would speak with you at this important time. We may speak different words and in different languages, but you will notice perhaps that the message is the same? Our message is a simple one. We wish to bring you an understanding of who you truly are and why you are there at this time, and in so doing, perhaps bring a measure of comfort to all of Humanity.

We wish only to help you wake up!

We wish only to be your support!

All information and Guidance that truly originates from the Light will only ever reflect the Love that is that Light...that is indeed you, as in a mirror! We will only ever offer you an understanding of a situation that is based on Love and support, and the message will always be one of encouragement...it will always be uplifting for Humanity.

You will always recognize this Truth when you are practicing discernment.

Do not listen with the mind Dear Ones!

Listen with the heart...hear with the heart...feel with the heart...always!

The heart will guide you in the right direction!

After receiving this channel, I suddenly understood the

significance of some experiences I have had very recently while trying to leave my body when I have been in an altered state of consciousness. As I explained to you earlier, I have only ever had a couple of negative experiences with this, and that was in the early days. They were simply entities residing in the lower astral planes of existence, and they were a nuisance, but in no way were they malevolent. I was sure then, and I still am that this was to show me that lower energies do in fact exist. I have not been bothered with them since. These latest entities though were very different in as much as they were very definitely not of human origin, and they were very obviously malevolent.

Thinking about this now, I may have also been given the understanding of another problem I have been experiencing. For some time now, I have been having difficulty actually getting off to sleep at night. I start to drift off countless times, and each time when I am almost asleep, something brings me back with a jolt, and I lie there wide awake again. This has become so troublesome that I have had to resort to a mild sleeping tablet, which simply activates my "sleep" switch. Although I dislike resorting to medication, this has bypassed the problem, and at least now I am able to get some sleep!

After speaking with Antoine, I now realize that these negative energies must have me on their "hit list." He explained to me that they do not want me to spread these messages in any way. They know that they can't trick me, so they are trying to intimidate and frighten me instead; however, it will not work with me...I will not enter into fear! Their tactics will just make me stronger and more determined than ever to spread these messages, which I know I receive from the Light. I know that this Light will always win out! They know that too of course, and that is why they are becoming desperate. If no fear or negativity remains in our world, these parasitic energies will have no more Human misery to feed from.

I asked Antoine why he did not warn me about what was going on with this earlier. I was gently reminded that I did not ask the questions! He is right of course...as always...I didn't! Why do I forget to do that? I guess I am still not used to the fact that any information I might need is so readily at hand. I was not really perturbed by what happened anyway; after all, I have had some very strange encounters over the years, to say the least, and I honestly did not suspect that I was being deliberately targeted for some kind of attack. I had no reason to, but I certainly know now! I also know that I have a lot of help at hand,

and that help will not allow me to be hurt in any way. You also have this help, whether you realize it or not! You only have to ask.

Antoine assures me that the Light will always be triumphant, and I will be able to handle anything that is thrown at me! My guides and Angels sat back during these encounters and did not intervene in my experiences. They say that it allowed me to see and feel how strong I am myself...without their help! It also allowed me to release some of that self-doubt and lack of self-confidence I have been struggling with throughout my life.

I am very much aware that the following accounts of these recent experiences will sound too far-fetched and too "out there" for some, and it was never my intention to include them in this writing, simply because I did not understand what was happening, and I did not want anyone to enter needlessly into a place of fear. I did not want to write about anything negative, but Lightcrow has now brought through this message, and he assures me that this is an important subject; he has asked me to include them here. Please believe me when I say that this was very real for me. Please believe me also when I say that I was not hurt at all in a physical sense, or in any other way for that matter.

With the first encounter, I thought perhaps that it was just some kind of an attachment, which I had somehow acquired, and it was now time for me to free myself from it; however, it is now my understanding that it was in fact, some form of psychic attack by some strange looking entity, in order to try to influence my thoughts and drain my energy. I don't know how long it had been there, but I am grateful that I found it and disposed of it accordingly; I think that I might have had just a tiny bit of help! It is interesting to note that I had also been suffering from an unexplained neck-ache and tiredness, which thankfully has now been largely resolved. This was obviously a physical manifestation of the attachment, and it is an excellent example of how attachments of all kinds, including our thoughts and our emotions can manifest as symptoms in our physical body.

The second encounter was simply an intimidation tactic designed to frighten me off.

This all just seems to be a part of my changing reality these days!

Journal: December 10th 2010

After my husband had left the room this morning, I felt

myself lapsing into an altered state of consciousness, and I became aware of intense pain at the back of my neck. I was not totally out of body, and as I reached around to feel my neck, I felt what I can only describe as a long thick tail, which obviously belonged to something...some sort of creature perhaps? I moved out of body and saw this worm-like "thing" biting into my neck. It was quite long and thick, and appeared to be attached to me with its mouth. I immediately tried to pull it off, but it let go of my neck and bit into my hand. It really hurt, and I became angry, so I grabbed hold of it by its tail with my other hand while it was still unattached to my neck. I actually wrestled with it, and then I flung it as far away from me as I could while screaming at it to "get, and never come back!" I remember seeing its teeth; they were huge and razor sharp.

Journal: March 13th 2011

As soon as my husband left the bedroom this morning, I started drifting into an altered state of consciousness. I became aware of a presence, and instinctively recognized it as a dark energy. I seemed to be paralyzed and could not move...not even in my Light Body. It was actually preventing me from leaving my body, and it would not allow me to see it either. It spoke to me in a threatening male voice, but afterwards, I had no memory of what it actually said.

When it first arrived, it patted down the sheets around me as though it was trying to make me comfortable. I could not see it, but I could feel it moving towards my head. By this time I was becoming really angry; I did not appreciate being unable to move at all!

I eventually summonsed up all of my strength, and that allowed me to break free from its hold. Finally, I felt myself rise up and out of my body, and then I swung around in my Light Body and grabbed hold of it. It was very strange looking; it had the body of a Human male, but the head of an animal...similar to that of a fox! I reached up to grab it and push it away from my physical head, and it bit me! I wrestled it out through the door, and then I flung it away from me onto the hallway floor. One of my little dogs was sitting outside my door, and he could obviously see us because he ducked out of the way and took off in fright. I screamed at it to get away from me, and to stay away and never come back, and then it disappeared through the closed front door.

I flew back into my physical body just as my husband

appeared with my breakfast.

This entity reminded me very much of some of the ancient images, which I have often seen depicted on Egyptian heliographic tablets.

Note: Both these incidents occurred while my husband was out of the room and away from me. Whoever these energies are, they are obviously cowardly, and they know better than to enter into his space!

While writing these journal entries, I remembered another encounter, which I had almost forgotten about, so I will tell you about it also. I experienced this one in June 2009. At the time, I thought that it was a bit strange, and of course I was a bit put off by it, but I did not attach too much importance to it.

As is often the case, it happened at night while I was in bed. I was obviously in an altered state of consciousness, but I knew where I was. There appeared to be a baby with me...fairly newborn. For some reason, I remember feeling great Love towards this baby. I slowly became aware of another presence, and I recognized it as being of a dark energy. It first showed itself to me as strands of a black and grey, metal-like material...not unlike curly bits of steel wool. This eventually transformed into the image of a very foreboding dark face. It reminded me of a pirate; very much like the one Johnny Depp portrays so beautifully in his pirate movies! It totally paralyzed me, and I was unable to move. The next thing that I remember, I was awake in my bed.

If anything like this ever happens to you, please do not be afraid. These beings simply perceive your Light as a threat to them, and they just want to stop you from seeking your Truth, through deception and intimidation. The moment you enter into fear, they have achieved their goal. They use a form of psychic attack, and they cannot hurt you physically. If you confront them, they will leave you alone. They would prefer not to have any kind of confrontation with you because your Light is much stronger than anything they can dish out, and they are very much aware of that fact. That is why they act in a cowardly way and do not want you to see them. It has been my experience that once they are found out…they run!

Now that I am aware of their presence, and I have been given an understanding of what is happening, and why it is happening, I can be far more vigilant.

CHAPTER SEVENTEEN

Guidance

Now, for the second time, I will attempt to write this chapter, which I hope may give you some understanding of how I receive my own guidance!

In addition to the encounters I have already shared with you, there have been times when I have received guidance specifically about something I have been experiencing on a personal level at the time. Mostly, this has been received through visions while I have been in an altered state of consciousness, or delivered to me while I have been out of body. Occasionally, for me at least, guidance can also be received by way of dreams. Some of these experiences have been so special that I would like to share them with you.

The first time I remember this happening was in 1997 when my life in general was very stressful. I really needed some direction, and I had been asking for some kind of guidance. This was received in the form of a vision while I was in an altered state of consciousness, and it happened at night, just as I was falling asleep.

When these visions are received by me, I view them through my third eye area, just like I would if I was watching a movie, but I can actually interact and communicate as well, even though I am aware that I am still in my physical body and lying in my bed.

Journal: January 2nd 1997

Last night I had an encounter with a spirit entity, who introduced himself as Phillip. He appeared to me in a colorful, yellow jester's costume with red and green on it, and he had a masculine, but humorous face. I asked him why he was in contact with me, and he replied that it was because he could help me at this time with some guidance. He told me that the best thing I could do at the moment was to find myself a "pet rock," and work with the energies from it.

I thought later on that he certainly was a jester, and the joke was probably on me! A pet rock? He had however, appeared to be highly evolved, and he was certainly quite serious about it when he was speaking to me. I decided that it couldn't hurt to at least try it! After a few minutes thinking about it, it occurred to me that he might be referring to crystals, and then it didn't sound so silly to me at all. I will purchase some crystals and endeavor to learn a bit more about them.

Note: This was the beginning of my continuing fascination with the crystal realm, and today, the use of my crystals is an integral part of my daily life.

Two days later I had another vision, and this one took place as I was drifting back to sleep early in the morning.

Journal: January 4ᵗʰ 1997

I was trying to get back to sleep after a disturbed night, but I could hear a female voice, so I asked if she was speaking to me. Suddenly, a woman appeared to me, and she said: Hello Robyn, my name is Donna, and I have come to give you some healing. She had a pretty face with blue eyes and fair skin, and her long, wavy, black hair was parted in the center. She was wearing a cream colored, short sleeved, midriff top, which was tied at the front, and harem-like, violet colored pants. A white towel was slung over one shoulder, and she was carrying a stone jar, which could have contained some sort of oil. I would say that she was about thirty years old.

I asked her if she was still alive and simply appearing

to me in spirit form, or whether she had actually passed over. She said that she had "died" fairly young in her last life, but I was not to worry about that. We spoke some more, but I can't remember what was said. Suddenly, she told me that she had forgotten to bring something for me that was very important, and she must go and get it, but she would be back. She did not appear to me again, at least not that I can remember. She may have returned while I slept, or perhaps she meant that she would come again at another time.

I remembered this morning that I have seen her before. One afternoon a few months ago while resting, I heard beautiful guitar music and a female voice singing, and then I saw this same woman sitting on a stool, playing the guitar and singing a song. There was a lot of background noise, like you would hear in a restaurant or such, but I could clearly hear the words of the song. It was a beautiful melody about how she had left her baby in Heaven to come to help.

Note: I now believe that she was trying to tell me that something had been forgotten, and my Doctor might have missed something. He had! I had been having trouble with my throat and neck for some time before I finally had a diagnosis. I believe that she was telling me about my thyroid tumor. I think perhaps Phillip may have been trying to do the same, but I just simply did not understand. I did know that it was very real though!

I have now learned to take much more notice of what my guides are saying to me when they appear. I now understand that there is always a reason for their visits. They have not once led me astray, and I trust them implicitly!

These days, they are able to connect with me more easily. They know that I fully understand what is happening and who they are now, so it is a much simpler process. They are more direct with their guidance, and they often just simply appear to me, and then say what they have to say! The most recent guidance concerning my health was in July 2010.

Since the surgical removal of my thyroid, I have had to ingest a daily thyroxin medication. Unfortunately, I have had ongoing health issues arising from this. My levels either rise too high, or they dip too low! There are many factors influencing the body's ability to utilize this medication properly, and my levels have never really been stable. Consequently, I have to submit to regular blood tests to keep the problem under control. I had been feeling really un-well for almost two weeks, and I seemed to be getting slowly worse. It felt to me like my levels were low, but I didn't think that it could be that because I had only had blood tests done about two months earlier, and everything was fine then. I decided that I probably should make an appointment with my Doctor anyway.

I was lying in bed half awake during the night when the same beautiful blonde haired woman, who had brought me the pink nappy pins appeared, and she stood directly in front of me. She simply told me that I needed more thyroxin, and then she disappeared!

I visited my doctor the next day and asked her to do more tests because I was feeling so un-well, and I thought perhaps that I might need a higher dose of medication. I felt that I couldn't share with her the reality of how I knew this, so I simply told her that I had a dream, and in the dream, a beautiful blonde haired woman told me that I needed more thyroxin! She looked at me a bit strangely, but happily obliged. When I visited her again a few days later to get the results, she looked at me strangely again, and then she just shook her head as she told me that my beautiful "dream" lady had been right!

My levels had dropped considerably, and they were far

too low.

No wonder I was feeling so un-well!

Journal: August 10th 1997

Vivid dreaming during the night, but I cannot remember what about! I was trying to get a bit more sleep after waking towards dawn when I became aware of a scene taking shape through my third eye vision...it was like looking through a tunnel. I could see what appeared to be a large expanse of calm, deep blue sea, and then the scene changed, and I could see a swimming pool full of clear, pale blue water. I was taken along the length of it, and I could clearly see the black lines for the swimming lanes painted on the bottom.

I was in awe at the depth of the blue color of the sea. I knew that I was in my bed, and I thought that I had actually exclaimed out loud, but my husband said that he didn't hear me say anything.

Note: I understood this to mean that the deep water, which I felt that I was drowning in at the time was becoming shallower, and things were beginning to become clearer for me.

This is in fact what did happen!

In the following account, I was actually given information for my own benefit from one of my spirit guides before I gained any sort of an understanding of what he was even talking about. I am still not absolutely sure about the meaning of this, but it is the only explanation I can come up with!

Journal: March 30th 2000

During the night, I became aware of a male spirit entity standing directly in front of me. He told me that I had now been granted six chances, and the records had been altered accordingly; then he simply just disappeared! I did not even have an opportunity to ask him what he meant by it.

Note: I was puzzled by this, and I continued to think about it. Eventually, I started to read a new book I had recently purchased. It was written by a well-known Psychic and Medium, and in this book she talks about how we write five potential exit points into our script, or blueprint before we incarnate here. When each of those points is reached, the Soul chooses whether to use it to return Home or not. It depends largely on whether we have achieved what we wanted to achieve here. Perhaps mine were all used up, but I needed to remain here to help, so I was granted one more opportunity to exit?

I really don't know!

Journal: March 10ᵗʰ 2001

I had another bad night last night; I could not get to sleep for the second consecutive night. At some point, I felt myself leaving my body, and I became aware of a weight above me. The female spirit entity had obviously been very close to me, and she was startled by my sudden appearance. She started to move away from me, but I asked her to please come back because I would like to talk with her. She said that her name was Mary, and she had been a member of an old family firm of accountants, but she had "died" young. She told me that now she helped keep the records on the other side, and she was very happy doing this work. She started telling me things about my future, like in a spiritual reading. She had a large script in front of her, and I realized that it was my records she was reading from...my Blueprint, or Life Chart!

Even though I tried to remember it all to bring back with me, I have forgotten most of it, but I do remember that I felt absolutely elated and uplifted by what she told me, and that feeling has remained with me. The one thing I do remember very clearly was towards the end of the encounter; she actually showed me part of my script. It very clearly told me that I would have a new home, and I would own it. I was so happy; I could feel myself smiling!

Note: I had been feeling really "stuck" where we were living, and I had been asking for some guidance about moving to a new location, and whether we would be able to afford another house if we did that. This encounter left me with a feeling of comfort, and the confidence to start moving forward again. Even though it would be another four years before we were able to make that move, I knew that it would happen, and that is what helped me cope with what was happening in my life at that time. I knew that I would get through it, and there was in fact, light at the end of the tunnel!

The following account is of a lucid dream, and it illustrates how information can be received in this way.

Journal: December 13th 2002

Lucid dream early this morning: I was shopping in some sort of arcade, and I am sure that I have dreamt of being there before. The shops were all on one level, and they had a very futuristic look about them; there appeared to be lots of glass and metal. I remember thinking that this was a special place I was visiting, and I wanted to buy some small thing to remember it by. I did buy something; I could remember what it was during the dream, but I can't now! I do remember though that I only had thirty dollars to spend. I came upon this very large shop with large expanses of glass from floor to ceiling, and I was completely mesmerized by what I saw through the windows.

There were the most amazing and unusual displays of handcrafted leather goods...wallets, bags and backpacks...all handcrafted with trimmings of leather thonging and beading. I have never seen designs like them. I noticed the shop was closed, but I dearly wanted to look inside. As I approached the glass door, it opened, and there stood an old school friend of mine. We were inseparable as young teenagers, and that is how she appeared to me. She told me that they were closed, but I could go in if I stayed with her. I asked her what she was doing there, and she replied that she was just there helping; I think she said that she was helping her Mother.

As I went inside, I noticed a few other people there. They were male, and they were what I perceived to be American Indians, but I could not see their faces because they were wearing very life-like masks, which depicted different native animals. One of these Indians spoke to me. He was wearing the mask of a brown bear over his face, and he told me that I was one of them once, and I could be again if I wanted to. A conversation took place between us, but unfortunately I have little memory of what was said. I remember looking up at some shelves, and there were all these beautiful little handcrafted, leather, drawstring pouches displayed on them. They were all packaged in little boxes with see-through lids. I was very drawn to them, and I expressed a wish to buy one to put my "stones" in. I guess that I must have been referring to my crystals?

He went to another shelf and took one down for me, but this one was different to the rest. It was golden in color, and quite exquisite! I told him that I really wanted it, but I did not have the twenty-five dollars required to buy it because I had already spent some of my money. He told me that he would keep it for me, and when I was ready, I could come back and claim it from him. As he said this, I remember having some sort of memory flash where I saw myself as an Indian with long black hair and dark skin. I don't remember anymore!

Note: I had no understanding of this at the time, but it is now quite obvious to me that this was very important information about my life purpose for this incarnation. I now believe that Indian to be Lightcrow, and although I have no memory of it, I think that I must have gone back fairly recently when I started working with him and retrieved that pouch he was holding for me!

This remains one of the most lucid dreams I have ever experienced.

You will no doubt realize by now that I have received much helpful information and personal guidance from the other side, and I will always be grateful for that. We all receive this guidance in some way or another, and this is very often by way of dreams. I would urge you to remain alert, and to take notice of your dreams because they often contain very helpful information. If you don't initially understand what the dream is telling you, simply keep thinking about it, and understanding will eventually filter through into your consciousness; you will eventually "get" it!

I am going to end this chapter on a slightly different note. I feel blessed to receive so much help from so many on the other side, but on this particular occasion, it happened to be my privilege and my pleasure to return the favor for a beautiful lost Soul, who actually needed my help!

Journal: April 12th 2007

I was out of body early this morning when I encountered a young woman, who reminded me very much of the images I have seen of Marilyn Monroe. She would have been in her early thirties, and she had a headband holding her chin length, blonde hair in place. She had blue eyes and clear skin with prominent make-up and bright lipstick, and she wore a melon colored twin-set with white pearls around her neck. She appeared happy enough, but she seemed unsure of where she was. She told me that she was caught under the "fuselage" and needed to feel Love again, but she couldn't find it. I told her that she needed to go Home to the Light now to find that, but she told me that she didn't know how. I told her that if she wanted me to, I would help her find the Light, and she would find all the Love she needed there.

I reached out and held her hand, and at exactly that moment she looked straight ahead and stared at something. As her face became illuminated with intense bright white light, she turned towards me and thanked me, and then she disappeared. When I looked further over to my left, I saw her re-appear. She was running up a wide, marble staircase with her hand on a black and gold hand rail, and then she just disappeared into the Light! I remember her skirt...it was very full, and it fell to just below her knees. She was also wearing black, flat shoes... 1950`s maybe?

I am guessing a plane crash.

Note: Although this is an everyday experience for my husband, spirit rescue is not something I have had a lot to do with, and I was extremely moved by this experience. I had the feeling that she had been waiting there for some time, not fully understanding what had happened to her. Finally, it must have been the realization that she was missing the Love from her life that had allowed her to seek help, and to move forward into the Light where her Loved Ones were waiting for her.

I feel so very blessed to have been that help.

CHAPTER EIGHTEEN

Time

I t was actually Antoine, who first spoke with me about the changes we will be experiencing within our perception of time, but it is now Lightcrow, who is going to expand upon that awareness for us.

Lightcrow

We welcome you once again Dear Ones,

We say to you: You might think that you understand how Time moves, but we tell you now that you do not yet truly understand this concept you term Time. We offer you a small, and perhaps a simplistic part of this understanding, simply so you will recognize the changes, or the symptoms as they begin to manifest in your world and within your Human consciousness; indeed, within your changing reality.

Time does not move Dear Ones! It is you who moves!

You move through time! It is in fact, your planet and you along with Her, which moves!

You think of time in linear terms…as a straight line, comprising past, present and future, and this is because your planet has existed within the concept of finite time where everything has a beginning and an end, but this is simply not the truth of it at all; indeed, the concept of Time might be more adequately presented to you as one comprising concentrical bands…placed one on top of the other, forming a spiral. These bands of time are infinite, and they simply become smaller and smaller until finally, they reach the place of "no-time"or"now- time," which is simply the Light, or the energy of the Higher dimensions. This is the place where Time simply collapses in on itself. As your planet evolves, and She raises Her consciousness along with yours, She is passing through this spiral, and this is the place within Time…this point of infinity that She is fast approaching. As She rises rapidly towards the higher dimensions, time for you on your planet is in effect beginning to collapse. You are reaching that point where it can no longer spiral out; that place of "no-time."

You are all familiar with the symbol of the spiral perhaps? This is a universal template of creation, and it is found in many forms throughout the entire universe. It is as such utilized by Mother Earth in many ways, including the simple pine cone. You are all familiar with this particular creation within your natural world perhaps?

We would ask you now to simply visualize this

perfect, beautiful pine cone, which is indeed, one of nature's many intricate gifts to you. You will notice that this pine cone is much broader in circumference at the base. This is where it has been grounded if you like, or attached to the physical life force...the pine tree. It is much denser and heavier here. As it has grown larger, it has spiraled up and outward towards the light. During this process, the pinnacle of the cone has become smaller in circumference and lighter in weight, in order to remain attached to the tree for as long as was necessary. Finally, it reached the point where it could no longer spiral out, and it simply remained static. This pine cone is not solid; it has what you might term small compartments...or pockets throughout its composition. An insect is able to enter into these spaces and move around, and then it can emerge again at will. Now we would simply ask you to think of these spaces as pockets of your Time, and to think of the insect as yourself!

It is indeed possible to enter into these pockets of times past, and also into pockets of times future if that is your choice. Some of you can consciously do this now, and you will understand the immense responsibility involved with this. All who eventually understand this concept must practice this sense of responsibility because every strand of possibility attached to your Human pathways already exists. Can you imagine the possibilities *Dear Ones?* You may re-enter a time when you were happiest, and simply observe it, or actually enter into it, and re-live it! You may also enter into a time and a situation where you would have preferred to have done things differently, and you may make amends. We tell you now that it is indeed quite possible to literally alter or "bend" Time! You do not need to create a time machine to do this Dear Ones!

You ARE the time machine!

More understanding of this concept will become available to you as you become more fully conscious and aware, and you have access to more of the subtle energies now washing onto your shores.

We hear many of you saying now that Time appears to be speeding up, and there doesn't seem to be enough hours in the day anymore. "Where has the time gone?" you ask! Your perception is correct! You all understand how the passage of time in the past has affected everything on your planet, including you. How could you not when you witness your children growing up and your hair turning grey, and perhaps also the deterioration of your health? This deterioration of the physical vehicle has been true for everything that exists in your world of matter because everything has existed within the denser energies of the lower vibrations...the lower dimensions where finite time exists...where everything has a beginning and an end.

We know that the concept we now offer you will be hard for many of you to grasp at this point, but we tell you now that all of Humanity will experience great change when you finally reach this place of "no time." There will be no deterioration of matter once this place has been reached. Time will stand still; there will simply be no time; there will only be "now!"

Can you imagine Dear Ones how this may affect your relationships with Mother Earth, and with each other?

You, as the Human species on your planet will eventually be carrying so much of your Light Body within that you will no longer have the need for a dense physical body, in order to experience your beloved Mother Earth. You will not grow old, and your health will not deteriorate; you will not "die" as you all eventually do now. In fact, dis-ease for all sentient beings on your planet will be non-existent. You will be able to remain there for much longer than is possible now, and when you choose to leave, you will simply do so in the Light Body you already occupy!

The time is almost at hand!

The time when the Truth will be told!

Your hard work will finally be rewarded, and you will have indeed created Heaven on Earth! We watch in amazement and wonder, and we hold your hands with our hands, and your hearts with our hearts.

What incredible Creators you are!

We say to you all: Well done!

I don't know about you, but lately I have been very aware of the time just flashing by! There really are not enough hours in the day for me. In the past when I retrieved something from my memory, it was just that – a memory. It seemed to me to be so long ago, and so far away that it was almost as though it had never happened. Often I felt totally unattached to it, but lately, I feel as though I could almost reach out and touch that memory, even if it is from forty or more years ago, and I thought that I had forgotten it. If I close my eyes and really focus on that memory, it is almost as though I am really there re-living it, and it seems to me that no time has passed at all!

I also have some small understanding of this concept of accessing pockets of time. I think that I may have actually experienced it firsthand. These experiences were totally unexpected and spontaneous, and they involved actual buildings, and the occupants from times past.

The first time that this happened to me was on my wedding night in Toowoomba in 1998. We spent the night in a beautiful, very old house, which was in the process of being restored. Our accommodation was in one of the rooms located in a recently finished wing at the very back of the house. This was a separate section, which was connected to the main house via a walkway. We found out afterwards that it had originally accommodated the children's classroom and the Nanny's quarters, and was fondly referred to as "The Children's Wing." I might add here that ours was the only room occupied that night.

This was probably one of the most incredible things that I have ever experienced.

Journal: October 6th 1998

We were very tired after our big day yesterday, and we were actually ready for sleep fairly early, but neither of us found the bed comfortable. The mattress was too hard for both of us, and I soon developed a backache. I slept fitfully until 1:30am. and finally got up and took some pain relief. I lay awake for ages, unable to get back to sleep, but I must have drifted off again because I was rudely awakened by loud voices. I thought that it was strange because I knew that we were the only guests in the wing. I figured that the noise must have been coming from the main house, but then I heard footsteps and laughter in the hallway right outside our room. I tried to pull myself fully awake because I thought perhaps someone might have gained access to our room, but as I became partially conscious, it was obvious to me that there was dead silence! I realized that I must have been hearing the voices and footsteps clairaudiently, so I simply slipped back into the place I had emerged from!

This time, I was aware of three distinct voices. Two of them were male, and it sounded to me as though the men were reasonably mature with well-educated Australian, or perhaps English accents. The third voice was female, and she had a very strong French accent. The woman sounded young, and I would say that she was rather promiscuous if the conversation I heard was anything to go by. They were now in the room next to us, and they were obviously going out somewhere because they were discussing whose bedroom they were going to come back to later! I listened for some time, and then I must have drifted off to sleep again.

I woke up about 6 a.m. and found my husband already awake. I asked him if he had been disturbed at all during the night. He said that he didn't have a good night because of the mattress and he had little sleep, but there had been no noise at all, and there certainly had not been any loud voices. I thought that I would check out the other rooms, just to be sure no-one had arrived during the night, but they were all still empty.

I realized then that I must have tapped into another time within the history of the house, and as I thought about it, I remembered that the girl who had shown us to our room had referred to the building as the original children's wing. Suddenly, it dawned on me that perhaps back in the time when the house was first built, the owners probably would have employed a Nanny, and it was quite possible that she was French; she would probably have been housed in this wing also.

I questioned the owner about it when she brought our breakfast into us, and she confirmed the fact that there had been Nannies employed back then, and they had been housed in the section we were in. Although she was unable to confirm whether one of them was French, she did say that it was quite possible because the name of the house was the original one, and it was in fact French; the original owners had strong French connections.

The second experience I had with this was only a couple of years ago, and it involved our present home. When we first arrived over five years ago at our new Tasmanian home, which is well over a hundred years old, we quickly became aware of the fact that we had a visitor, who was keeping a close eye on our attempts at restoration. She is a young woman, who appears to us dressed in period clothing with her dark hair pulled up. She checks in from time to time to give us her approval, and she can often be seen standing at the back bedroom window watching us while we are outside in the orchard with the dogs. She is aware that we can see her, but she is a friendly presence, and she simply smiles at us. This house was built by the original publican for his daughter and her family, and we believe that it is she who visits. She does not bother us in any way whatsoever; in fact, we quite enjoy her visits!

The subsequent owners lovingly occupied the house for over fifty years, and they raised their family here. I have mentioned Kitty and Harold before, and I am reasonably sure that somehow I managed to tap into a time when this house was their home.

Journal: February 21st 2007

This was not a dream I had last night. It was very strange because I thought that I was only a spectator, but I was visible to them as well. I was out of body, but I remained in my house, and I saw spirit people walking around in it; they were occupied with their daily activities, and they were bathed in a soft golden, white glow. The most memorable person was an older, plumpish, white-haired woman, who appeared from the kitchen wearing an old-fashioned apron. I noticed that there was a door to the kitchen; there is none there now, but you can see the marks from the hinges where one was previously. The furniture in the house was not mine either. She came out of the kitchen and closed the door behind her, and then she went across the hall and into the back bedroom. She came back out again and headed back into the kitchen. I stood at my bedroom door fascinated! She reappeared in the hallway, and that is when she came face to face with me!

She could obviously see me too because she suddenly appeared startled, and then she acknowledged me. I told her who I was, and she told me her name was Kitty. I remember thinking how strange that was because we had owned a cat by that name. Then I saw a young girl appear. She had blonde curly hair, and she was wearing a red cardigan. She skipped through the hallway right past me and smiled at me as she went…she was obviously not bothered by my presence at all! I know I spoke to Kitty for a while, but I have no memory of what was said. I was so excited when I woke up this morning…I couldn't wait to tell my husband about it!

Note: I was not aware that there had been a woman called Kitty living in this house until well after this experience, and I really have a very limited understanding of what happened that night. I know that the experience was real and I was in my house, but so were they, obviously in a time past. In a way I can understand how I was able to see them because I was out of body, but if I was the intruder into their time, how on earth were they able to see me?

I simply don't know!

I don't know whether this next, final account for this chapter actually fits into the category of Time or not, but I would like to include it here. I have a very strong suspicion that this Soul is going to enter my physical life in a very personal way sometime in the future.

Journal: May 11th 2003

I felt myself entering an altered state early this morning, and I was aware that I was leaving my physical body. I decided to stay close to my body and remain aware of my room around me…I enjoyed the feeling of just floating there! Suddenly, a spirit entity flung itself at me; it was in such a hurry to get to me that it almost sent me off the bed! It was a very young boy with straight black hair and very dark eyes, but he had a fairly light complexion. He was about five years old, and he had an elfish, cheeky grin.

He just kept smiling at me, and I felt so connected to him. I knew that I should recognize him somehow, but I didn't! His facial expression changed, and his smile started to drop when he realized that I didn't recognize him, so I said that I was sorry, but I didn't know his name. Just at that moment, the thought struck me that his name was Peter David. As I said his name, he brightened up again, and said: Yes…4lbs. 5ozs!

He immediately passed right through me and disappeared!

Note: Something tells me that I have not seen the last of this beautiful, loving Soul!

CHAPTER NINETEEN

Past Lives

The first time I remember experiencing past life recall was in fact, many years ago, and it actually happened quite spontaneously. I was sitting quietly outside, enjoying the sunshine while admiring the beautiful views from our hilltop home. My husband and I had been experiencing a lot of stress caused by interference in our personal lives by other people, and I was wondering how on earth we were going to cope with all these problems, which were beginning to impact on our relationship. I began to wonder just why we felt the way we did about each other when it was so obviously going to be such a hard road for us to follow. It would have been so much easier to have just given up, and walked away from each other.

As I closed my eyes and allowed my mind to drift, I began to receive a vision. I saw a young woman, who I knew to be me, standing outside a beautiful, two storied, stone house; somehow, I knew that this house was in the French countryside, and that it was mine. Suddenly, as I lifted my hand to open the heavy, wooden front door and walk inside, my awareness shifted into my other self. As I entered, I immediately recognized the interior of the house, as well as the skillfully made and beautifully hand carved, wooden furniture, which was scattered throughout. There was a man there, who I recognized as my husband…in this lifetime, as well as in that lifetime.

Somehow, I knew that he had crafted all the beautiful furniture himself, and he was in fact, well known as a furniture maker. I even had the understanding that his furniture is still known in France to-day. I brought back with me, the knowledge of his full name, as well as the Christian name of our son, who I might add could possibly be still alive on the Earth plane to-day! Strangely, I brought back no knowledge of my own Christian name. I also had the understanding that this was just before the Second World War, and my husband had later enlisted as a pilot. Unfortunately, his plane had been shot down, and he did not survive WWII. As I re-emerged into this reality, I experienced an immense sense of sadness and loss.

It is interesting to note that he has the same dark coloring that is typically French in this lifetime as well, and his Mother in this lifetime was also French! He has always had some memory of being a pilot, and can actually remember fragments of what happened to him. He was injured when his plane was shot down; he used his parachute, and was helped by allied troops when he landed. They were burrowed down in trenches, but were overrun by German soldiers, and he was shot through the chest. He incarnated this time around with a permanent reminder of that last incarnation; he has a very large, mole-like birthmark near the centre of his back; this marks the exit wound from the bullet, which so tragically took his life.

Not long after I received this vision, I experienced a lucid dream. I was in a bar, and I was dressed in the fashion of the 1940`s with my dark hair pulled up in a French roll. I picked up my drink (I think it was a martini) and turned around, and as I did so, I could see my handsome husband sitting over against the back wall, waiting for me to come to him. Our eyes met, and I was overcome with Love and longing for him; I knew that we had not seen each other for some time. He had a cigarette in his hand, and he was dressed in his air force uniform. He was on a short leave and was unable to come to our home, so somehow I had managed to go to him. I remember walking towards him, and as I did so, I was brought back into this reality, and I also understood that this was the last time I was to see him in that lifetime. I woke up in tears, experiencing a feeling of indescribable loss, which remained with me all day.

It was after these two experiences that I truly understood our feelings for each other in this lifetime, and I also understood that the Love we shared would see us through anything. We had finally found each other again on the Earth plane, and we had another opportunity to continue our story together because it had been taken away from us so tragically the last time around.

The story never ends.

The Love never ends.

I do not know how I passed over to the other side at the end of that incarnation, which quite obviously encompassed WWII, so I do not know whether it was tragic or not, but I do know that I incarnated again fairly soon after the war because my birth year this time around is 1952, and realistically speaking, I could barely have reached middle age in that lifetime.

I also had the following dream in 1999, which was not long after I had the previous experiences.

Journal: April 5th 1999

Very vivid dream last night: I was a younger woman, perhaps in my late 30`s, and I was wearing a somber green dress with my dark hair pulled back in a French roll. I was on some sort of a train with a lot of other people, and the fear was palpable…I felt very afraid!

While I was sitting with a group of people talking, two men came over and stood either side of the window with a piece of dark cloth stretched between them. I understood that if they did that, the soldiers would not be able to see us when they shone their strong lights through the windows. Suddenly, I found myself in another seat near another window, and I was looking down at a small wooden sculpture of an animal in my hands. (I can't remember which animal!) A man, who told me that he was a sculptor was admiring it, but he said that it was slightly out of context.

I had been given the sculpture by a friend, and I loved it, but I suddenly decided that I was going to try and improve on it. For some reason the material became malleable in my hands, and I reduced it to a pulp, but then realized that I did not possess the artistic ability to re-do it. All of a sudden, I seemed to have forgotten all about the sculpture, and instead, I was intent on teaching those around me about psychic protection. I remember looking around me for a safer seat to sit in because I was afraid of being seen where I was near the window, and then I moved seats.

The next thing I remember, I was obviously leaving the train because I was collecting my few belongings, and I was saying to some people that they were letting me go because they had found out that I did own my home, just as I had tried to explain to them when they had herded me on to the train. Everyone wished me luck, and then I saw myself standing at the side of the train tracks with some other people, who had also been put off the train.

The countryside was green and lush, and we appeared to be in the middle of nowhere. I can remember the huge, shiny, black train whooshing past me. It was very long, and it had lots of carriages attached to it. There were many soldiers standing at intervals along the train tracks, and they were dressed in very dark uniforms; I think they were black and a dark tan, or khaki. They also wore long, shiny, black leather boots, and they held big, long rifles in their hands.

I spoke to the woman beside me, and I asked her how on earth we were going to get back home. We had no idea how far we had travelled, or even which country we were in. I made a lame attempt at humor as I told her that I would have to get new doors for my house before I could live there again because they had smashed them in when they took me away.

I realized then that I was probably going to be some sort of refugee in a foreign country.

We were escorted by soldiers, and we seemed to walk for miles. Eventually, we came to a very old looking town, and we were taken into a building where some men were standing behind a large counter; it looked like it was an official building of some kind. I walked past some of the men to the end of the counter where an older man with a kind, happy, round face was smiling at me; he had unruly, graying hair. He took my documents from me and stamped them, and then he said that he hoped I enjoyed living in Italy!

He pointed to another part of the building and told me to go there. I was still with the woman from earlier, and as we walked past the counter, we saw that there was food laid out for all of us; I was very hungry and ate well.

I don't remember anymore.

Note: I was watching this as in a movie, but I knew

that the woman was me, and I was experiencing all of her emotions at the same time.

Very recently, I experienced another insight into this ongoing journey with my husband, which I am sure I was meant to pass on to him, perhaps to give him a better understanding of his relationship with one aspect of his life today.

It has also given me a much better understanding of him!

As I have mentioned before, he has been a volunteer Fire-Fighter for many years. This is his passion, which in my opinion can sometimes border on obsession! Because he was diagnosed with Multiple Sclerosis seventeen years ago, just a few years after we met, he has slowly had to wind down his activities and pace himself, so he does not become overtired and unwell, and suffer a relapse.

I have never understood why he could not just leave the callouts to someone else when he was feeling too tired to respond, especially at night. He has never been able to give me an explanation as to why this is; he just says that the need in him to respond is too strong to ignore.

It is interesting to note that the full understanding of this has come at a time when he is finally ready to let it all go, and enjoy the time he has left here without feeling the need to be responsible for others in this way.

I think perhaps that this particular debt has finally been repaid.

Journal: May 9th 2011

Last night I had a lucid dream...I was actually experiencing this dream. I was standing outside a very old house, and I was wearing an old style dress, which reminded me of women's clothing depicted in old American western movies. The house was wooden, and quite crude in structure, but it was my house. There was a small dirt courtyard, and across from the courtyard there was another larger structure, which looked like a large barn-type building with a very high roofline and wide open doors. There was a crude set of steps leading up to a large platform, which was higher up inside the building. It reminded me of some sort of sawmill, or factory. There was machinery of some sort in there, and also a lot of sawdust strewn all over the dirt floor. I understood what it all was at the time!

I looked up and spoke to my husband, who I recognized as being my husband in this lifetime as well.

He was standing on a crude ladder cleaning the chimney of the house, and he told me that he had cleaned the fireplace inside also. I looked over and saw a young lad, who I recognized as one of our employees, carrying a type of bucket containing ash and coals. My husband yelled out to him, and he told him to empty the contents of the bucket in the courtyard near the building, and then to get on with his other work. I told my husband that was a silly thing to do because there was sawdust everywhere, and it might catch alight! He was very rude and arrogant to me, and he yelled at me. He told me that it would not catch alight, and to just shut up and mind my own business.

As I stood and watched, the whole building erupted into flames, and then it burned right down to the ground. There was a lot of screaming, and people were badly burned; there were also deaths. The victims had been working in the building, and they were unable to escape because the fire had erupted near the doors where the coals were dumped. Some people came to help, and I remember someone being put on a crude type of stretcher and taken away in the back of some sort of cart.

My husband was very arrogant about the whole thing, and he remained adamant that he had not been responsible for any of it. He did not seem to be affected by it at all…on the other hand, I was totally distraught.

It is of course quite ironical that I would choose a Fire-Fighter as my husband in this lifetime because I have always experienced an intense fear of fire. With the exception of a garage fire a number of years ago, there has never been anything happen during this lifetime that would logically explain that fear. Even now when he empties and cleans out our wood heaters, I have to make sure that he has disposed of the ash safely, and at least now I understand why I am so fanatical about this; however, it is not the only reason I am afraid of fire, and I was given an insight into this quite a few years ago.

I was having an afternoon rest, and I was almost asleep when I saw myself standing next to a crude clothesline; I was hanging some sheets over the line. I was perhaps in my thirties with long, wavy, light brown hair, and I was wearing a long, blue, old fashioned gathered skirt and a white peasant style, long sleeved blouse. There was a young blonde haired girl playing in the grass beside me. I knew that she was my daughter, and she was about six years old.

Suddenly, two men appeared, and they grabbed hold of me and forcefully led me away. My daughter was screaming, and I was overcome with fear because she was being left there on her own.

The next thing I saw horrified me! I was tied to a wooden stake with fire all around me, and I knew that it would not be too long before it reached me. Just for a moment, my consciousness flew into this other "me," and as I looked out at the people gathered around to watch the spectacle, I recognized my husband from this lifetime standing there. I realized that he was a part of my life at that time also, and we had been secretly seeing each other for some time. He was powerless to help me, and his face was filled with hopelessness and despair, but I understood that he had to keep quiet, in order for him to be there to look after my daughter because she was his daughter too.

The fire had reached me, and I was so utterly filled with fear and horror that I abruptly pulled myself out of the vision, and sat up in my bed with my heart racing.

It has become very obvious to me that Antoine is absolutely correct when he says that each lifetime is a continuation of the same story…our story, and that story never ends. It is also very obvious to me that we interact with the same Souls, over and over again as we play out that story, and in so doing, we learn what we have come here to learn.

We learn how to Love.

There have been other dreams and visions during which I know I have been experiencing other lifetimes. Within the level of my more recent understanding of multidimensionality, I am not quite sure if these are my memories, or if they are the memories I have access to of the many incarnations of those other aspects of my Soul, but it really does not matter to me because I know that we are all a part of the one consciousness…the one Soul, and we are all me anyway!

Journal: March 30th 2005

I had a very vivid dream last night. I was a young male with long, dirty looking hair, and I was wearing a short, dirty, cream colored tunic with leather thonging laced around the middle; I had similar, crudely made boots on my feet. I was with other males dressed the same way as me, and we were carrying long spears.

We were being chased by a tribe of men, who were dressed in a similar fashion, and as we were running across a lightly forested area, they appeared en-mass over the crest of a hill behind us. We ran towards what appeared to be an old wooden church where we hoped we would be able to take shelter, and perhaps barricade ourselves in.

We heaved open the heavy wooden door, but inside there were only wooden beams, and they were crisscrossing the floor about half way up. The only place to hide was in an area that was only accessible by a small opening, and it was too small for us to go through. We realized that the situation was hopeless, and we were probably more at risk in there than outside, so we turned back the way we had come. We ran towards an area where there were some small stone walls, and we decided to crouch down behind them. We hoped that we wouldn't be seen by our pursuers, but we were prepared to fight for our lives there if necessary.

As the others descended upon us, I realized that it was hopeless, and I was probably going to be killed if I stayed there. As I looked around me, I spied a very large tree, which had sweeping branches with foliage reaching right down to the ground. I quietly slipped under the foliage, and I hid there until it was all over. Nobody looked for me there...they obviously thought that they had killed everyone.

I was too afraid to move for quite some time, but eventually someone lifted the foliage and found me there. It was a man from a nearby town, and he took me home with him.

My life had been spared this time.

Journal: November 23rd 2005

Very early this morning, I became aware of looking at a young woman, who I knew to be me, but I was also experiencing her consciousness. I was sitting down at a desk, and there was a man on the other side of it. He was dressed in old style clothes, and he was speaking to me. He called me Miss. Mason, and he asked me if I was ready to sit for the examination now. I asked him what name he had just called me, and he said: Miss. Mason... Helen...that is you isn't it? I said: Excuse me, but what year is this?

I was very confused because I actually thought that it was me in this reality sitting there. He replied: Why, it's 1853 of course!

Journal: November 29th 2006

I was having a rest this afternoon when I suddenly

realized that I was out of body. I rolled off the bed and looked around at everything in my room...I felt totally elated! I wondered if I would be able to see a reflection of myself in the mirror, so I went and stood in front of my dressing table. To my utter amazement, I saw that my reflection was exactly as it is in the physical state, but as I stood there, my features began to blur and slowly start to change. I was transformed into a much older woman, but then I continued to change form, like a shape shifter! I became two different men; one was short and stocky with glasses, and he had a balding head and a moustache. I know that I also transformed into another woman, but I can't remember what these other forms looked like. I am assuming that these were perhaps some of my identities in other lives. As I looked further into the mirror, the scene changed, and I became aware of two puppets beating each other up. They looked like Punch and Judy, and they were dressed in really bright colors of red and green and yellow. I found myself laughing at their antics, and then I decided to bounce around the room in my Light Body!

Note: I don't know the significance of the puppets, except to say that I probably just needed to lighten up and relax a little. I certainly had a good laugh, and I absolutely love moving around in my Light Body. I always feel as excited as a child in a lolly shop!

Perhaps I was also being reminded that it is always the Light Body animating the physical body. The Soul is always in charge…it is always in the driver's seat!

The physical body is simply the puppet.

I would like to end this chapter by sharing with you a very special visitation, which I felt very privileged to have experienced.

In 2003, as I was drifting off to sleep one night, I had a visit from an older, distinguished looking gentleman, who was dressed in very old fashioned clothing. He couldn't stop hugging and kissing me because he was so excited, and then he showed me an entry in a very old book, which he manifested in front of me…it could have been some sort of marriage registry. The script was also very old fashioned, and it read:

JONES Jeremiah

GORDON Rose.

JULY 12th 1821

Was he my Jeremiah, and I his Rose?

CHAPTER TWENTY

The Last Word...Magic and Miracles

lthough I am assured that my work with Antoine and Lightcrow will be ongoing, they have indicated to me that this will be the final communication from them that I am to include in this book. They feel that the amount of information contained within these pages is enough for the mind to comprehend and fully digest at this time. As our time progresses, there will be more information filtering through from them for me to share with you.

They want us to understand that we have all chosen to be in physical form on the Earth Plane in what they term these "magical times," even though it may not appear to be that way for many of us at the moment.

We are now being asked to show our hand so to speak, and to begin to put our unique piece of the puzzle for the creation of the New World into place. We are being called into active service for Mother Earth and for all of Humanity. Those of us who already have an understanding of what is taking place are now being asked to hold the hands of those who don't yet understand, so as to lessen the impact of their fear, and in so doing, to help them through these troubled times. This will allow them to enter with us into the magic of the Light, which will then help to facilitate the process of their own spiritual awakening.

We have many helpers at this time, and they would simply ask us to invite them into our lives with Love. They will provide the support we need to complete this process; they would simply remind us that we are never alone.

Lightcrow

We welcome you once again Dear Ones,

We have told you this before, and we will now tell you again: You are all what you would term Magicians; you simply have to remember this!

Throughout the history of your time, the Angelic Realm has been privileged to be of service to Humanity, and it continues to be so; indeed, there are many volumes of accounts written, and many words spoken throughout your world about these most magical interventions. The logical Human mind, and especially the minds of those within your scientific fraternities have not yet sought and found an adequate explanation for such events, but we tell you now that you will all be experiencing, or witnessing these interventions in a more profound way than ever before. When this magic is eventually manifesting all around you...you will no longer be able to simply ignore it as many of you have done in the past. You will have no option but to begin to open your minds up to another possibility...a different kind of possibility, in order to understand what has taken place. Once the mind has been opened and the questions have been asked, the spiritual path is then accessed with the heart.

The Angels and many other Light Beings are now entering into your Human consciousness in a profound way, in order to play their part in this magical evolvement that you are creating; indeed, to honor their contract with you. In so doing, they will help to facilitate the Awakening for many of you. They will now be arriving in increasing numbers to show you that there is another side to all of this; there is not just the cleansing process that you see taking place all around you. They are coming to show you that there is indeed magic waiting for you when you finally step into the Light. They will do this by helping you to see yourselves for who you truly are right now...powerful beings of Light...just as they are, and capable of entering into and changing an outcome yourself…simply by utilizing your own powerful healing energy.

The one you know as Jesus was indeed a Teacher and a Healer, but he was also what you might term a Master Lightworker. He walked the Earth plane at a time when Humanity was in great need of hope, and He showed by example what all Human Beings are capable of. You will now be shown again, and this time you will all understand.

You will all understand the Truth!

This will be especially evident at this time within your scientific and medical fraternities. They will now be learning to access and use the healing energies from the Light on a conscious level. Many of them are doing this already on a sub-conscious level…they just don't realize it! They are accessing this healing energy from the Source through their Light Body, and once they witness the medical miracles, which will now be orchestrated upon your planet, they will begin to open their minds to this understanding. The healing Angels are now connecting to them, and guiding their hands and their hearts in a way that can no longer be ignored by them. Expected tragic outcomes will simply not eventuate! Unexpected healing of body and mind will take place instead, and many cures for your Human dis-eases will now be realized. You are already starting to see this happen in your world. Keep your eyes and ears and your hearts open, and you will witness this in and around your own lives as well, and not just within the physical body, but also within the healing of your emotions and relationships.

We will tell you now that in order to facilitate some of these miracles, especially where the energy is designed to radiate out into the consciousness of Humanity on a large scale, there are many who have entered into contracts with the Angelic Realm, and they will now step forward to play their part in this process. It is time! Many people, including their Loved Ones will possibly perceive these beautiful, loving Souls as what they might term the "victims" of these scenarios.

This is simply not the truth of it at all!

We would simply remind you all that there is always a reason for everything that happens. Everything is as it should be; indeed, nothing is ever added, and nothing is ever taken away. Everything that happens in your life has your consent, so to speak. It is a part of your purpose for being there; it is a part of your piece of the puzzle; it is a part of your contract. You are there at this time because you have something to contribute to this process, and you have willingly and lovingly agreed to do that.

These special Souls; the ones who have answered this particular call to service understand that when a tragedy strikes any individual, the effects also impact on everyone around them; indeed, their family and their friends, but also those who help and support them in a myriad of different ways...personally and professionally. When what you would term a miracle occurs within the healing of the physical body or mind, it also touches those same people; it affects those people, if only in a subtle way. All who witness it are changed by it to some degree, and when they are unable to make any sense of what has happened with the logical mind, they will begin to open up the mind with the heart, and begin to ask the questions.

You can see how this would work perhaps?

This is also important work on another level; it facilitates the connection of the Human Family in some way. Even though they may not understand this yet, remember also that the Loved Ones, who are working through this process with these special Souls have also made this contract...they are all in this together.

Indeed, you are all in this together.

Eventually, this understanding of the spiritual aspects,

as well as the physical aspects of healing will allow the blending of the sciences to take place. The opposing sciences will eventually merge, and they will complement each other; they will bring balance to each other in a way that will be beneficial to all of Humanity.

Magical times are indeed upon you Dear Ones. Allow this magic to weave its way throughout your lives. Do not be afraid of these miracles…do not be afraid of the magic. You are all Magicians, and once again we tell you: You are finally creating your Heaven on Earth.

Dance in the Light Dear Ones, and experience the magic waiting for you within!

We have enjoyed communicating with you so much throughout this process, and we thank you for your ear. We look forward to speaking with you again.

We are greatly honored to be of service to you; indeed, to all of Humanity, and to Mother Earth Herself.

We continue to hold your hands with our hands, and your Hearts with our Hearts.

We send you much Love.

The following words from Lightcrow were meant specifically for me, but I would like to share them with you if I may.

My beloved Brother, I have enjoyed this small part of our journey together so much...riding the hills and the plains with you once again.

Just as it has always been.

Just as it will always be.

I have not left your side; our work together is not yet done.

Rest now Dear One; we will speak again.

I honor you and the work we do together.

About the same time this channel was received by me, I had an experience at Home in the higher dimensions of reality that I would like to share with you. It validates for me the fact that these healing energies are washing onto our planet right now...at this very moment in our time.

I have already mentioned my friend, who is a gifted Healer. I have been aware for some time now that we both meet up at Home in the higher dimensions of reality at night while operating in our Light Bodies. I have brought some of the memory of this back with me before, which I have shared with her, but after this latest experience, it is now evident to me that we actually work together there, helping to manifest certain aspects of Home in the physical world. These aspects are designed to help Humanity at this time, and many of them are of course working with the Teaching and Healing energies.

For her own reasons, she has chosen not to have any conscious memory of what she does while at Home, and as Antoine explained to me, she works totally with her intuition and her Faith. She holds the healing knowledge of The Ancient Ones within her Light Body, and this has been accumulated over many lifetimes.

Perhaps the best way I can explain to you what is happening in this area is to share with you some information that Antoine brought through for me to pass on to her, and the best way to do this is simply to write it exactly as I did for her.

I have her permission to do this, of course.

My Account of What I Experienced on the Other Side

We were together in a room in some sort of healing facility, and there were a lot of people there. They were sitting in straight backed chairs, and they were seated in rows. There seemed to be a lot more female energies than male. I wonder now if that has something to do with the fact that in the physical state, women are traditionally far more susceptible to emotional and physical abuse than men. They were holding onto the sides of the seats on the chairs with their hands, and they kept their backs straight. They had some sort if thin slippers on their feet, and they were stretching their feet right out and tapping in time to some music. First they were tapping the whole foot, then the toes, then the heels, and then the sides of the feet – a number of times each time. The floor was a wooden one.

The music was not just any music; it seemed to be comprised of some kind of music scale in conjunction with tone frequency, and had a vibration or harmonic that extended at the end of each different note. It reminded me of xylophone music with bells attached! Very hard to describe, but I have heard music on the other side before because everything there emits music and sings in beautiful tones. The singing isn't actually with voices – it is more like sound vibration and tone frequency. Unfortunately, I don't have the words to describe it adequately. It is really something that has to be experienced firsthand.

Have you ever heard someone play a handsaw?

While I was witnessing this healing session take place, I had the knowledge that everything could be healed with different types of sounds or music. You were the healer helping them to do this…I was the spectator, who was simply there watching. You were out amongst them and interacting with them; you knew exactly what you were doing. You had absolutely no difficulty with teaching this concept. I had the understanding that this in some way helped the alignment and cleansing of the Light Body.

I don't know if this is something you already know about on a conscious level, or whether this is a healing concept you practice on the other side, which will be new to us here, and you are going to help develop it and bring it through.

I am definitely not here to tell you that this is what you have to do. I have simply been asked to pass on this account of what you were doing there. The rest is for you to work out, and I know that you are very capable of doing that.

Whatever choice you make will be the right one.

Information I Passed on with Help from Antoine

Apparently, when we leave here, there will often be some residue left from illness and trauma associated with the experience of our recent physical life. This will be left as negative fragments, which remain attached to, or are embedded in the Soul or Light Body by certain vibrational frequencies. These can be aspects of emotional or physical trauma. These aspects have to be gently and lovingly transformed, and then cleared from our Light Body before we can move on and do what we want to do on the other side. There are facilities on the other side with wonderful Healers to help facilitate this process, and many of them are here on the Earth Plane at this particular time as well. They are working double shifts!

You are obviously one of these. Apparently you have been working with the healing stream of energy for eons. It is just simply who you are, and you hold a vast amount of knowledge. You have held back a lot of this knowledge until now because certain aspects of that knowledge are in some way only used for healing when there is a large amount of Light Essence held within the physical body, as in ancient times, or when there is no physical body attached to the Soul or Light Body, as in the higher planes of consciousness. With the original plan in place allowing for the possibility that Mother Earth might shed Humanity at some point during Her evolvement, you incarnated with the understanding that it would not be needed here unless we chose to evolve with her; that decision had not been made at that point. Now everything has changed because we as the Human species chose to change it. We have chosen to evolve with Mother

Earth instead of leaving Her and incarnating again somewhere else in the universe.

Because of this, we basically have to re-write our future. We are doing a lot of that on the other side when we visit at night, and we are also working out what we need to manifest on the physical plane right now, in order to help Humanity through this shift of consciousness. Everything for use here has to be worked out and perfected on the other side first...in etheric form...before it can filter through and manifest in the physical world. Our bodies are changing, and they will be starting to hold a lot more of our spiritual Essence from this point on, just like they did in ancient times when we existed along with Mother Earth within the lighter energies, so obviously some of the other, higher energy methods of healing will be appropriate to use here now.

Even though the Soul brings back all the knowledge it needs with it each time it returns to the physical body, unless you actually have conscious memory of what you have been doing during the night while there, you have to wait for it to filter through the layers of your etheric body into your Human consciousness. Even though this is happening faster now, it still takes time. Most people never remember what they were doing there, and they receive the information and guidance from the Soul itself to help them, by way of simply knowing something and recognizing it is a Truth. This is a reflection of Home. Sometimes the information is sent via messengers; these are people who do have conscious memory, or who have the ability to access the records on the other side on your behalf.

You have chosen not to have conscious memory of what you do there. I can't give you a reason for that and neither apparently can Antoine. Only your Soul holds that knowledge, and considering the fact that we can change things now if we want to, I would say that you have a very valid reason why you haven't done that. That is not to say of course that you can't do that sometime in the future if you choose to.

This is why you are receiving information from other sources at this time; we are the messengers, who have chosen to help you in this way. I have been asked to share this information with you, in order to let you know that it is alright to live your Truth here now if you choose to. Do not be afraid to step out and share your knowledge; it is going to be needed in an ever increasing way.

I am sitting with Antoine while writing this, and as you have probably already guessed, a lot of this insight has been his. He has asked me to tell you that you will have the opportunity to bring different concepts of healing through; you will be able to develop them in a way that can be used here if you choose to. He says that it is now possible to move in another direction…away from your Teachers. You can move away from that energy now…you already have the knowledge to do this yourself. You will be the Teacher. He also asks me to gently advise you to be especially aware of practicing discernment with those around you if you do. He warns of the shadow being very active around activities such as this, and it can be very cleverly disguised.

I have the understanding from him that the message you received about having time for yourself and nurturing yourself now is a valid one, but it is not only referring to doing that in a personal way; it is also referring to the nurturing of the passion you hold within, for your work…your healing work. You know what aspect that is. You will find that the two go hand in hand because in fact, nurturing is your Essence. It is who you are…it is your Truth.

One will follow the other.

Antoine stresses that the choice is always yours. Any information passed on to you is exactly that…information that you might find useful. It is always entirely up to you what you do with it. What you choose not to do this time around will simply be picked up again at another point somewhere on your journey.

It will be done.

Music is the Key!

Throughout the process of this writing, I have been in constant communication with Antoine; he never leaves my side of course! I thought perhaps that because he had the first word in this written work, it might also be appropriate for him to have the last word.

Often, as I am watching a world event on television, or thinking about something that is happening somewhere, he will start providing me with information about it. This is mainly for my understanding of a situation as it arises, but with his permission, I thought that I would share some of it with you.

A little glimpse into our future, so to speak.

I am sure that many of you watched the recent British Royal Wedding as it unfolded on our television screens in a state of rapt enjoyment. It really was a fairy-tale manifesting in this reality. I have it on good authority that the Love between these two is real. It is not staged, as has often been the case on many other Royal Wedding occasions; it is the real deal! In fact, I did not really have to be told that because I could feel it myself, and I am sure that many of you could as well…it was palpable!

Antoine shared with me the fact that the British monarchy was actually due to collapse…to end; the new energies would simply not support them any longer. Apparently, there has been much greed and self-service involved around them in the past, and much has been hidden, even from many of the Royals themselves.

These two young, very beautiful and special Souls have come to help on our planet, and they have consciously chosen to change that outcome and create something different instead. They understood that they would be in a position to transform those negative energies of the past into positive ones for the future - for the good of Humanity. Instead of allowing the Monarchy to fall, they are resurrecting it and supporting it, and leading it in a different direction. Their intention is to use the enormous power their position provides, and the wealth that goes hand in hand with that power, for the good of Humanity. They both possess the integrity to do this; they both know no other way of being. In fact, they have already been doing this on a smaller scale for some time. Similar situations will now be arising all over our planet.

What good news this is!

Anything that serves to separate instead of unite will not be supported by the new energies, so I am wondering if those people wanting to see Australia become a Republic might be somewhat disappointed, or does "Taking Back Your Power and Responsibility for Self" on a national level apply here?

It will be interesting to see what we create with this one, won't it?

Something that we will also be witnessing more and more of at this time is the connection between Souls in ways that were in the past, unacceptable within our societies, especially within our western societies and religions, and this was because of the mainly judgmental way of thinking. This was supported by the old heavier energies. Antoine says that these relationships will now be supported by the new, lighter energies, which are now washing on to our planet…the gentle energies of Healing and Unconditional Love. People can now choose to be with whom we might term a Soulmate without any judgment attached.

The time for judgment is now simply finished.

One of these aspects of change is the growing

disregard for age differences between people within intimate relationships. Personally, I am so pleased and uplifted to finally see this occurring. I have always believed that if people truly Love each other, age should not matter...no exceptions! Within the new, higher consciousness, people will be able to live their lives in any way they choose to, without fear of ostracization, or retribution by society.

Another phenomenon is that of same sex partnerships. Antoine assures me that in our future it will be commonplace for these loving relationships to nurture our young. They will be able to offer a unique understanding of who we truly are. They will understand that in spiritual form there is no gender. We can choose to be whoever we wish to be, and we bring the aspects of that through with us, in order to experience what we have chosen to experience while here. Where Love is concerned, gender in physical form is of no importance. Nothing is of real importance except the Love we share. We truly are all equal, and we are connected to each other through the one Essence – the Essence of Love - the Light.

It is truly only the Love that matters.

I am heartened to hear his words on these subjects because it gives me great hope for our future as the

Human race.

Perhaps the greatest miracle of all will finally occur.

Perhaps we can truly Love each other after all.

I pray so.

EPILOGUE

A lthough sometimes challenging, the experience of writing this book has been both a pleasure and a privilege. In many ways, it has also been one of the greatest gifts I could have ever given to myself. As a child, and as a young adult, I always felt that I could never express who I truly was. I felt very controlled by what I always perceived as my parents expectations of me, as well as those of society in general, and I developed a sense of very low self-esteem. I always believed that everyone else was in some way better than me because that was the message I was always receiving. This belief continued throughout much of my adulthood, so this writing has been a cathartic experience for me. I received the understanding from Spirit when I was first diagnosed with thyroid cancer that the reason this particular cancer had manifested in my physical body was because I had not spoken my Truth for most of my life. I have now finally been able to express who I truly am, through sharing my reality with you.

Many years ago, at a time when I was questioning a great deal about my life in general, I received the following channel about reality. I did not understand where it had come from at the time, but I knew that these words were not mine, and even though I did not hear a voice as such, I also knew that I had not imagined them.

"It is important to remember that this is not your true home...not your true reality. This world is but a stage, and you have chosen to act out your life here. You are but actors on this stage for this lifetime. You have been given free will, and it is up to you whether you are good actors, or bad actors. One thing is certain; all experience in this lifetime has been chosen by you to enhance your spiritual growth, and whether you judge it as good or bad, it is all just experience. You have many unseen helpers waiting in the wings, and you only have to invite them into your lives with Love."

There are two things that have become crystal clear to me during this process. The first: It is a great privilege to be here experiencing the Earth Plane at this important time, and to be able to help our beloved Mother Earth in this evolutionary process. This is not just Her evolution, but ours as well. Not everyone gets to do this; it was our choice. We offered our service to the universe, and that service was gratefully accepted because we possess the ability to help.

We all have our unique role to play.

Part of my role is to bring these messages to you. I now understand of course that this is why I have been experiencing this lifetime within a level of consciousness that would allow me to share our changing reality with you at this time…from a first-hand perspective. That does not make me more than you, and it does not make me less than you…it simply means that I am fulfilling my role. Each one of us is of equal value…none is more or less than the rest, and we are all in this together.

I have been guided every inch of the way with this work, and I trust my guidance implicitly; however, I feel that one of the most important messages to be received at this time is the one addressing discernment. This is the one that spoke to my heart. The message is clear! Please do not give your power away to anyone, or anything! Listen to your Higher Self …your Soul, because you hold all the knowledge you need within you. Observe and take notice of what is happening in your own reality. By all means listen to what others have to say if you choose to. There is much helpful information and guidance filtering through to us at this time, but please do not just accept everything that is said and done by others at face value. The shadow is more active than ever, and it is so easy to become confused, and to give your power away to someone else.

Seek your Truth, but please practice discernment!

I would urge you to practice it with this work as well. The messages I have received are simply being relayed to you in the hope that they may help you remember who you truly are, and why you are here at this time. It is entirely up to you what you do with them. If something in these words speaks to your heart…to your Soul, and you recognize it as a part of your own Truth; then please take notice of it, and claim it as your own. It could very well be a message meant specifically for you.

If it does not, then I would ask you to make no judgment…simply let it be.

The second thing that has become clear to me is that although we are here for a specific reason at this time, we are first and foremost, Human Beings experiencing the physical world, and all that it has to offer us. This in itself is a great privilege and cause for celebration! Although I sometimes wish that I could stay at Home in the higher dimensions when I visit, I was told early in my communications with Antoine that I have much more to experience here before my Blueprint is complete, and I intend to have a fun time doing it! I do enjoy being

Human! I love my Human relationships with my family and my friends, and I love my animal companions. I enjoy my glass or two of red wine! Although sometimes challenging, I love my Human life, and I know that I am here to enjoy that life.

I want to experience more of what Mother Earth has to offer, so I have decided to do just that. I have always wanted to travel, but I have never really been in the position to make that a reality. I had in the past believed that there were higher priorities in my life. I see everything from a different perspective now, so I am just going to step outside that box, and do it anyway.

It will work out somehow!

I cannot in all honesty receive these messages and not be changed by them…not use them in my own life in some way. My intention is to consciously live my life within my Truth to my highest capability, and to live it now because not one of us really knows when we are scheduled to make our exit from this beautiful planet we call Mother Earth, and return Home…to our true Home.

I would simply urge you to do the same!

I send you much Love.

CPSIA information can be obtained
at www.ICGtesting.com
Printed in the USA
BVHW040235251021
619810BV00024B/601